THE NEWCOMER'S GUIDE TO WINNING LOCAL ELECTIONS

Terry A. Amrhein

Writers Club Press

San Jose New York Lincoln Shanghai

The Newcomer's Guide to Winning Local Elections

Published by Writers Club Press
an imprint of iUniverse.com, Inc.

For information address:
iUniverse.com, Inc.
620 North 48th Street
Suite 201
Lincoln, NE 68504-3467
www.iuniverse.com

ISBN: 0-595-00991-3

Printed in the United States of America

This book is dedicated to my lovely wife and best friend Cindy, without whom, it can truly be said, this book would not have been possible.

CONTENTS

CHAPTER 1- 1

DEDICATION, STRENGTH AND ENDURANCE

CHAPTER 2- 7

DEVELOPING CAMPAIGN ISSUES AND STRATEGIES

 Where to Begin

 Narrowing the Focus

 Presenting the Issues

 Accumulating Your Tools

 Know Your Community

 Nomination

 Primary Elections

 Deciding When to Run

CHAPTER 3- 23

DOING DOOR TO DOOR CAMPAIGNING POUNDING THE PAVEMENT

 Handout Material, Paper Handouts and Palm Cards

 Planning the Door to Door Effort

CHAPTER 4- 35

ROAD SIGNS, POUNDING HOLES IN THE EARTH

 Where to put road signs

 Professionally Printed Signs

Taking Pictures for Road Signs
Installing the Road Signs
Where to Get the Signs

CHAPTER 5- 43
DEVELOPING THE FLYER
  Bulk Mail
  Mailing to Each Voter or Each Household
  Overcoming the "Tendency to Toss"
  Developing the Flyer
  Printing and Mailing the Flyer

CHAPTER 6- 59
OTHER EFFECTIVE STRATEGIES
  Press Releases
  Letter to the Editor
  Personal Recommendations
  Community Events
  Campaign Trinkets
  Newspaper and TV Ads

CHAPTER 7- 67
CAMPAIGN FINANCES
  Using Your Own Money
  Ask Your Strong Supporters
  Having a Yard Sale
  Things that Don't Work
  Duties of the Treasurer
  How Much Will the Campaign Cost

CHAPTER 8- 77
PUTTING IT ALL TOGETHER

CHAPTER 9- 83
  ELECTION DAY

CHAPTER 10- 87
  SO, IT'S FINALLY OVER

APPENDIX- 91
  NEW YORK STATE ELECTION LAW, IN SUMMARY

ABOUT THE AUTHOR 101

PREFACE

In 1993, I became campaign manager for my wife, Cindy, on her quest to become Town Justice in the small Town of Ballston in Saratoga County, New York. How Cindy became involved in politics was completely by happenstance. A friend called Cindy one August evening and asked if she would like to run for Town Justice. Since the incumbent party had run unopposed for many years, we thought the competition would be good. After all, we thought, this is America and we're supposed to have a choice. Our friendly caller, however, neglected to inform us that Cindy would be endorsed by the Democratic Party. In a town which has three Republicans for every Democrat, the hopes of winning an election as a Democrat was dim at best. Three long and arduous election campaigns later, however, in 1996, Cindy became the first Democrat elected in the town in 20 years and the first woman Town Justice ever. During those election campaigns, I learned some important and useful information which may be helpful to the "Newcomer" entering the election arena. I write this handbook in the hopes that some of our experiences can lend a helping hand to those who have the strength and endurance to undertake running for the first time and, prehaps, against the "Favorite"party.

I've tried to present the information I have in a humorous, down to earth and entertaining fashion, to help keep the reader from becoming too bored in what can be a boring subject; political campaigning. I've included many short personal experiences (and whimsical tales) that Cindy and I had as we progressed through the campaigns. I've also tried to present the information in as short and concise manner as I can so the "Newcomer" candidate can obtain the information that he/she needs as effortlessly as possible and get on with the campaigning. I sincerely hope that what I have learned is helpful to you. Best of luck.

ACKNOWLEDGEMENTS

No one writes a book, even a small one, by themselves. My great thanks goes to my "favorite" Mother-in-Law, Agnes Barile, who spent hours reviewing the book and whose help was indispensable during the campaigns.

Special thanks also to Jean Ford, Commissioner of Elections in Saratoga County and Bill Fruci, Deputy Commissioner, for graciously consenting to review the appendix on the New York State Election Law.

1

DEDICATION, STRENGTH AND ENDURANCE

In 1993, my wife Cindy became a "Newcomer" to winning local elections. She ran as the Democratic Candidate for Town Justice in a small town in Upstate New York. I was her campaign chairman. In our town, the "Favorite" party, the Republicans, outnumber the Democratics by three to one. We had little chance of winning. However, four years later, after three long and arduous campaigns, Cindy became the first Democrat elected in over 20 years and the first woman Town Justice ever! This guidebook tells how a "Newcomer" can win local elections, even against the "Favorite" party. But let's start from the beginning, what it takes to be a good candidate.

As an "Newcomer", there are many hardships and miseries you will probably experience in your fight to be elected. You should have a realistic first hand description of what campaigning as an "Newcomer" is like. After you have read this chapter, if you're still willing to become a candidate, then you can continue with the rest of the book. If you say however, that you really don't think you're up to all this, then I'd advise you to save yourself a lot of agony and don't run. Everything in this chapter is real, there is nothing sugar coated and nothing exaggerated. Just the facts!

To Run or Not to Run—That is the Question:

1. IF YOU THINK YOU ARE GOING TO RUN ONCE AND WIN, THEN DO NOT RUN!

Unless you're running with the "Favorite" party, you are probably not going to win your first campaign as a "Newcomer". There are several reasons for this, none of which have anything to do with you personally, although this may be difficult to accept at first. It has nothing to do  with your ability or your qualifications. Some of the reasons for an unsuccessful campaign are:

-You are not well known, because you are not with the "Favorite" Party;

-You are not a viable candidate-YET; and

-Voter apathy or fear of change, the voters are going to blindly vote for the "Favorites".

To win, you MUST be prepared to run more than once. My review of the local elections in my town over the past 25 years revealed that almost every challenger ran only once, then quit! Only nine challengers ran more than once for the same office, although 91 candidates were elected during this period. Only one challenger actually was elected after his first campaign, and this was only by eight votes! You probably won't be so lucky.

When Cindy and I began our first campaign, I did not realize that our main chore during this first effort was to make the opposition really sweat. In this, we were successful. We campaigned hard and vigorously. We knocked on doors, we sent out flyers, we put up signs, and we participated in community activities. You see, we foolishly thought we were going to win the first time. Even though, in our minds, we knew the prospects were slim, we got caught up in the emotions of it all and felt in our hearts we should win. After all, Cindy **was** the best candidate. We did not win, but we gave it our very best effort and we did make the "Favorite" Party really sweat. We made them work hard to keep us with us. They were not used to having opposition, so when we ran, the opposition actually had to campaign. For the first time in years, the Town became alive during the local election. We put up a good fight and lost by only about 200 votes. Although Cindy did not win the election, she was becoming known and transforming into a viable candidate—a threat for the next election.

2. IF YOU ARE NOT WILLING TO WORK FOUR TO SIX HOURS PER DAY, PLUS AT LEAST EIGHT HOURS ON WEEKENDS BETWEEN JUNE AND NOVEMBER, THEN DO NOT RUN!

Most of us work full time. To add another four hours per day to your work schedule is a hardship. It is grueling, but an absolute necessity. BE PREPARED to extend your day and forget about a social life!

In 1995, Cindy ran again for Town Justice and lost. We both worked twice as hard as we had in the 1993 campaign. When the election was over, Cindy and I both collapsed. We were exhausted both physically and mentally. Our body's immune systems were vulnerable and we both came down with a flu that never seemed to end (but it did force us to stay in bed—which wasn't necessarily a bad thing!). We both knew that the work had to be done, election day is not going to wait until you have the time to complete all the work. It was extremely difficult to keep up the pace, you must be dedicated—-you gotta love it!

3. IF YOU DO NOT HAVE A TEAM OF 10 OR 12 PEOPLE WHO CAN HELP YOU WHENEVER YOU NEED THEM, THEN DO NOT RUN!

Winning an election as a Newcomer is not a one or two person job. You are going to need help, and LOTS of it! Not only is it impossible for a couple people to do everything, but you will literally go mad in the process. Tap your resources—friends, family and disgruntled local citizens, just to name a few.

When Cindy and I decided to campaign, we were very fortunate. Cindy had family in the area who were eager to help her get elected. Cindy's mother, father, sister and brothers worked endless hours helping us do the myriad of chores that had to be done. We also had a host of friends who volunteered to assist us. Amazingly, after three campaigns, these people were still our friends. Cindy's family had no choice, they still were family—but they still continued to love us, voluntarily! Additionally, a few local people, unhappy with the state of affairs in our town, volunteered to help. It did not take long for these people to become our friends. Working so closely together, day after day after day, you cannot help but become friends—their unhappiness with the local government became our unhappiness, and vice versa.

Regardless of where you get help, you must make it known that you are running for office and that you need help. Asking for help is not a sign of weakness. You will find that many people are happy to help; it is exciting for them to be involved in a political campaign. People are eager to assist. One rule of thumb, however, if you don't ask, you won't get the help. Don't be afraid to ask, it certainly cannot hurt.

4. IF YOU ARE THE TYPE OF PERSON WHO CANNOT TAKE DEFEAT, THEN DO NOT RUN!

Chances are you will not win your first time running. You may not win the second or third time either, but keep trying. Defeat is difficult.

It hurts to lose. It is also frustrating when you do not win when you have the most qualified candidate and you have worked so hard for so many months. Defeat is difficult to overcome, but my mamma always said, "Suffering builds character and time heals all wounds." You will go through a sort of grieving process. Feel free to grieve, then let it die and begin again. Never lose hope. The sun will come up tomorrow. There is always another election year and a seat to be had for someone willing to fight.

5. IF YOU CANNOT ASK FRIENDS AND FAMILY AND STRANGERS FOR MONEY, THEN DO NOT RUN!

Money is the sustenance of all campaigns. Without money, your campaign will die an unhappy death. Unless you are independently wealthy, you will need to get funds from campaign contributions. The best and easiest way to get money is from friends and family. Even strangers will give you money, if you ask right. Do not be afraid to ask, you will be surprised. It is awkward and uncomfortable to ask people for money. You almost feel like a beggar. Just tell yourself, it is for a good cause—YOU and better government!

Now we come to the conclusion of this critical chapter. I ask you, do you think I am exaggerating? Well, I am not. If you cannot handle any one of the things I have outlined above, DO NOT RUN as a "Newcomer" unless you are running with the "Favorite" party. If you are strong enough and good enough, then, by God, people will like you. Just remember, if at first you don't succeed, try, try again. If you have read this chapter and you still desire to run for office as an "Newcomer", then go to Chapter 2, Strategies. Let the fun begin...

2

DEVELOPING CAMPAIGN ISSUES
AND STRATEGIES

The Issues:

There are two HUGE tasks that your campaign strategies must accomplish. First, determine what issues are "hot and what are not"; second, decide how to best promote the issues and the candidates to get votes. Once you accomplish this, you have overcome a big hurdle.

For Town Justices in New York and most other states, issues are not a concern. Judicial candidates are not like other candidates. They cannot support or endorse issues or other candidates. Judicial candidates MUST remain politically neutral and independent. They must administer the law fairly and equitably to all citizens. Apparently, when Cindy ran, her opponent was not aware of these requirements. He boasted on his campaign signs that he was a "Republican Justice". I never did find out what that meant, who was the Democratic Justice? We picked up on this issue and ran with it—we campaigned on the fact that the law required judicial candidates to remain politically neutral. The only other real issue the Town Justice can campaign on is qualifications. Cindy was a practicing attorney, while her opponent was a retired insurance sales-man. There are subtleties within the qualifications issue, however. Cindy is a woman in the prime of her career. Her opponent was an elderly gentlemen whose career was at an end. Cindy's femininity and abilities might appeal to the women's rights minded voter and to more open minded men. The juxtaposition of the two candidates could work in our favor, but we had to be careful. We couldn't just come out and say "Vote for Cindy because she's a woman and in the prime of her career", we had to be more subtle than that. Our solution was as subtle as the problem. You'll learn more about our solution in a later chapter.

Candidates, other than judicial, can campaign on issues. The prob-lem, however, is deciphering the issues and deciding which ones to use in your campaign. How is this to be accomplished? One great way, is to have a party, everyone loves a party. I call it the "Campaign Issues Party". Invite friends, family and, of course, members of the community who are unhappy with the local government. At the party, have fun, but never lose focus of its purpose. First, identify all the issues and/or concerns in the community. Discuss each issue thoroughly. Do not for-get the subtle issues, such as age, occupation, looks and gender. Try to identify every aspect that will help generate a successful campaign, as well as those that might adversely affect the candidate. Someone should write the issues down as they are discussed, probably the campaign manager, since he does everything else anyway. A blackboard, or flip chart is very useful for this. Writing down the issues allows everyone to see them as they are discussed and helps keep the group focused on the purpose of the party. Also, writing down the issues provides a record for use later in the campaign. If the issues aren't recorded, take it from experience, later on you'll only remember that someone had a great idea, if only you could remember what it was. Finally, don't forget to ask for campaign contributions before the party breaks up.

Aside from focusing on the issues, the Campaign Issues Party also serves another vital purpose. Although they may not know it at the time, the people in attendance will form the basis for your campaign team, those 10 or 12 people you will need to assist you do the thousands of tasks that must be done. By attending the party, they have already become a part of your campaign. They have formulated your strategies and have become players and contributors to your campaign. Who can resist helping after they developed your campaign strategy? They will eagerly want to help you because if you win, they win. Everyone loves to be a part of the winning team, and you will definitely need their help.

Where do you Begin to Identify and Develop the Issues?-

In my Town, which is much like many other small towns, the Town Government has taken on a form and character all its own. For example, employees of the Town are often relatives of the elected officials (how convenient!); resolutions are passed almost unanimously in each and every Town meeting because the board convenes just before each "official" meeting to conduct the "real" business in private. If this sounds like your local government, you may want to consider using these issues in your campaign.

Town budgets are always a good source of fuel to fire up your campaign. How are the budgets prepared? How are the numbers derived? Where are the funds going to come from to support the itemized costs? What happens at the "public" meetings regarding these budget proposals? Is the public even aware of such meetings? Who attends them?. Is there ever any opposition to the budget proposals? Does the budget add up and balance, both literally and figuratively? You can find a plethora of issues regarding the budget.

Of course, there are always the issues of taxes, property assessments and road work that make good topics of discussion and generate fervor.

The makeup of the board is also another issue to consider. Does the Board consist of all members of the same party or is there a fair and accurate representation of the community on the Board? How about the Board members themselves? Are they qualified individuals or just those who happen to be in the good graces of the "Favorite" Party?

At your Campaign Issues Party, you will doubtlessly uncover an endless variety of topics. Remember, though, you cannot campaign on all the issues; you must narrow the issues and focus only on those that are most likely to excite the voting community to get them to vote, and vote for YOU.

Narrowing the Focus of Your Campaign Issues-

After your Campaign Issues Party, you will have plenty of issues to contemplate, but which ones should you chose? As you are cleaning up the mess from the party, you will have time to think. You cannot campaign on all the issues. Your time and funds are limited and the attention of the public is not that great; they can only handle a couple issues at a time. The attention span of most adults will last about as long as a TV commercial. Too many issues will also dilute the main ones and actually cause you to lose votes. This is a bad thing! Pick issues that are less likely to have conflicting views, ones almost everyone will want to support. You may want to reconvene your Campaign Issues Party group to help you narrow your focus. The campaign chairman should write down the pros and cons of each issue and then you can eliminate those issues that pose a risk or which you feel uncomfortable supporting. Pick solid issues where the established party is vulnerable. Also don't forget to save the reasons for selecting or rejecting an issue. Later on, you may start second guessing yourself and you may want to know what you were thinking at the time. Once you have selected your two or three issues, run with them.

Presenting the Issues:

After you have decided which issues to use in your campaign, you'll need to consider how best to present the issues to the voters.

Flyers mailed to registered voters are a good method to use to discuss issues. Getting the voters to read the flyers is a whole other problem. The flyer must be designed to grab the attention of the reader quickly and present the issue briefly, yet concisely. How many times have you thrown away political advertisements? How often have you read every word of political literature that was mailed to you? Get my point? There are many forms of advertising that get the point across with very few words; use cartoons, pictures, tables and charts. A "compare and contrast" method is excellent. For example: taxes in your community versus those in surrounding communities can be artfully communicated with a table or chart. A catchy headline and cartoon will grab the readers attention and force them to continue reading. Words of explanation are not necessary. Just how you should communicate your message should be discussed at your Campaign Issues Parties. Write down all the ideas concerning how the issues should be presented. You'll need these ideas and thoughts when it actually comes time to create the flyer.

Accumulating Your Tools of the Trade (Your Bag of Tricks):

Everybody needs tools to do their job; a plumber brings his pipe wrenches; a doctor brings his medical instruments to surgery (hopefully); politicians must also bring their tools to the campaign trail. The invaluable tools that a campaign manager and candidate MUST have in order to conduct a campaign are
-a detailed and accurate local map; AND
-a data base of registered voters.
These tools are critical, yet they are not difficult to obtain. A local map might be available at a commercial store, a grocery store, or a quickie market like X-Mart, Seven-Eleven or Cumberland Farms.

Another source of maps is your local Town, Village or City Hall. These maps will be indispensable in conducting door-to-door campaigns; deciding where the most populated areas are in the community; and many other issues that may arise, as we will see later.

The data base of registered voters is an absolute necessity. It is every bit as valuable as the map. It must be a computerized data base, a hard copy (printout) of the registered voters will not suffice. A computerized data base can be manipulated in any fashion you desire. For example, if you are campaigning door-to-door, you can sort the data base by street address. The campaigner can simply march down the street, knock on those doors with registered voters and avoid the houses where no one votes. You can create a mailing list and specifically target newly regis-tered voters or voters registered with a specific party. In this way, you can send flyers to only those voters you desire. You can also arrange the mailing labels by Zip Code. The Post Office requires bulk mailings to be arranged this way. This will save a lot of time over sorting the mail by hand. You MUST be able to manipulate the data base. If you are not computer literate, then find a couple of people who can do the job and be sure to invite them to your campaign planning parties.

Where do you get the data base you ask? In New York, you can obtain the data base from the Data Processing Center in the County Government Offices where you reside. In other states, a similar com-puterized voter data base is probably available for the local government. The name of the department may vary from county to county; you can inquire with your local County Board of Elections, which is in the phone book. There is, however, a cost for the data base. In 1993, when Cindy first ran, the data base for approximately 3,500 registered voters cost about $200 to $300, which, for us, was prohibitively expensive. As a result, we could only afford a hard copy of the registered voters. We did not have the time or the manpower to sort the data which was listed alphabetically by voter by district. Our campaign staff, went to every house on every street, not knowing whether the household contained registered voters or not. This was a tremendous amount of lost energy, time and effort, but we had no choice. In 1995, the law was amended, requiring that such lists be made available to the public at a "reasonable fee". Literally, overnight, the cost went from over $200 to about $12. I was the first in line! In 1996, the cost in New York was about .25¢ (1/4 cent) per registered voter; the cost for a data base containing 5,000 names and other vital voter information was about $12, the best money you will ever spend. When I got the data base I felt like Hercules; so much power at the touch of a button—I was unstoppable!

The data base provides a wealth of information. For example, the data base may give you the name, address and telephone number of every locally registered voter. The data base may also tell you when the voters registered and give a voting history of the last few elections (it doesn't tell you who they voted for, just whether or not they voted). Just think of the power at your fingertips! If you want, you can concentrate only on those voters who have voted in the last election, or last two elections. You can specifically target newly registered voters or you can target registered voters to a specific party or geographical location. The possibilities are endless. Well, almost.

In 1996, when Cindy and I organized our door-to-door campaigning, we sorted the data to target only those homes with newly registered voters. We decided that new voters were either young or new to the community and were less likely to be tied to the "Favorite" party. Furthermore, we had been doing door-to-door for the last three years and pretty much covered every house in the community. Unless they lived under a rock, or were new to the community, these voters were aware of Cindy. So, we concentrated our efforts where it would have the greatest effect. Without the data base, we would not have been able to use this strategy.

Yes indeed, the data base and map are POWERFUL tools. Don't leave home without them.

Know Your Community

It helps to know your community. How many registered Republicans are there compared to registered Democrats? How many are registered with the "Independence", "Liberal" or other party. How many are registered but did not specify a party? What district has the highest number of Republicans? Which district has the largest number of Democrats? All of this information will help you plan your campaign strategy. Also look at previous elections. Past election results are available from the Board of Elections and can easily be obtained by completing a Freedom of Information Law (FOIL) request. Find out which districts traditionally have been the strongest supporters of the "Favorite" Party. These districts probably still are their strongest supporters. Also, see if you can discover issues of particular interest in a district. Use these areas of interest in you campaign strategy.

In 1993, after our first campaign, we only took one district out of seven in our community. Although we came close in some of the other districts, we lost by a wide margin in two very strong Republican areas. We saved the data and used it in our next campaign. We knew where we had to concentrate to win and we concentrated our efforts in that area. Cindy especially concentrated her efforts in these districts since the voters like to meet the candidate's personally.

After your first campaign, you will accumulate a wealth of information. You will know where you did well and where you did not. This is why it is imperative not to give up after the first try. You are just a fledgling your first time out, learning how to soar.

When Cindy ran in 1996, we knew we needed to win the Democratic vote and most of the other non-Republican votes. We fashioned our campaign toward the Democrats and Independents who seem to be growing in number and toward those voters who seemed apathetic in the past. We knew where the highest concentration of Democrats were located. Using the data base and the map, we sorted the registered voters by party, district and street. We concentrated first in the districts with the most Democrats. We then concentrated heavily in those districts of the community where Cindy lost by large margins in her last campaign try. We also focused on newly registered voters. As the 1996 campaign came to a close, there wasn't a house in the community that didn't know who Cindy was and that she was a viable candidate in the upcoming election. Cindy even commented to me that when she walked into the local grocery store or gas station, people approached her with recognition and support. Although she said it was a strange feeling, deep down inside, I know she was loving the notoriety.

Another method of obtaining information about the community is to poll the residents regarding their concerns. This may take some time but can provide valuable information. The poll can be conducted by telephone. Choose registered voters and ask them what is their major concerns about their community. This should enable you to obtain sufficient information to get an adequate sampling of the community. Make sure you limit your requests to only one or two major concerns, otherwise you will be inundated with data that is too voluminous and broad to decipher. It also sends a message to the voter, that you are listening to your constituents, you care, and you intend to do something about their problems. In essence, you are there to help them.

All the information you gather about your community will be invaluable to you. Without it, you will be campaigning blind. The information you accumulate will not provide you with 20/20 vision, but it will allow you to see fuzzy images.

Nomination-General Elections:

Before you can run in an election, you must be nominated by a party. How is this done? Each state has its own requirements so you MUST check the laws in your state. The local Board of Elections is a good place to start.

If you are a member of the Minority Party, i.e. not the "Favorite", contact your local committee chairman. You can get the name and number of the Minority Party Chairman in your town or community from your County Board of Elections. Let the chairman know you are interested in running. Most Minority Parties are starving for qualified candidates and will eagerly accept your offer. Even if you are not a member of such party, chances are pretty good that they will endorse your candidacy.

In my town, for many, many years, the Republican candidates ran unopposed in all the local elections. Since they had such a stronghold in the town, no one came forward to challenge them. That was until 1993. I assume it was voter apathy or just plain ignorance that prevented anyone from challenging this one party system. Or, perhaps, it was the fear of losing that prevented viable candidates from coming forward. But, these reasons should not stop you from running if you can pass the tests presented in Chapter 1. Persistence pays off and the public may not be as apathetic or unconcerned as you think.

Getting nominated by the "Favorite" party is not so easy. Although I have never had the fortune to be part of the "Favorites", I have the opinion that to become a candidate with the Favorite Party you must show dedication and loyalty to the party for a considerable time. I guess all candidates must pay they dues some way, either you work hard for the "Favorites" for a long time before you are nominated as a "Newcomer" or you're nominated by the Minority Party but have to work very hard to get elected as a "Newcomer". I can attest to one thing though, there is nothing more satisfying than being elected as a "Newcomer" from the Minority Party.

Once a party has agreed to endorse you, your candidacy must then become "official". This is generally done by a caucus or petition, the process may varies somewhat from state to state. Special time frames apply when each process must be completed. (see Appendix on the New York State Election Law). A caucus is basically a meeting of the party members. Candidates are nominated and a vote is taken. The majority rules. You then sign an acceptance form and file it with the County Board of Elections. You are then an "official" candidate. It is that simple.

The Petition process is somewhat more tedious than the caucus. A certain number of signatures are required on a Petition designating the candidate(s) (see Appendix regarding New York State Election Law). If the nomination is for a candidacy in an established party (i.e. Republic, Democrat, etc.), then the signatures must be from registered voters in that party. The Petitions are then filed with the County Board of Elections and if there are no successful challenges to the Petitions, you are then the "official" candidate for that party.

There are other strategies, however, that you can use to get your name before the voters. You can get nominated by more than one party. All parties, once established, must select their candidates by either caucus or petition. You can contact the chairman of one of the smaller parties you feel will most likely support you. Some of the less dominant parties (i.e. Conservative, Liberal, Independence, Right to Life) often have candidates for state and national elections, but few, if any, candidates at the local level. These parties will more than likely welcome your offer to run on their line, assuming your philosophies coincide. Endorsing candidates at the local level provides these less dominant parties with a "presence" in the community. This gives them incentive to support you, and gives you another line on the ballot. It is definitely a mutually beneficial relationship. So, do not be afraid to ask.

Another way to get your name on the ballot, in New York and some other states, is to create your own independent party. To do this you must accumulate a sufficient number of signatures on a Nominating Petition (see Appendix regarding Election Law). Unlike one of the major parties, the signatures need only be of a registered voter, regardless of party affiliation. The petition form can be obtained from your County Board of Election. Once you have accumulated the required number of signatures, you must then file the petition with the County Board of Elections. If no successful objections are made, you have then created a new party and have "officially" become that party's candidate. This is a difficult way to get on the ballot. It does have its advantages, though. When circulating the petition, you are actually doing something very akin to door-to-door campaigning, just a little earlier than usual. Additionally, those people who sign your petition are likely to remember you when it comes time to cast their votes.

Selecting a party with which to run is a personal decision. However, do not feel as though you must limit yourself to only one party. You can be endorsed by multiple parties. Such endorsements have certain advantages. First, it puts your name on the ballot in more than one place and it provides you with some degree of credibility. People will see that you have been endorsed by more than one party and subconsciously conclude that you must be a good candidate to receive multiple party backing.

Secondly, it provides voters who are strong party supporters an opportunity to vote for you without having to vote on their traditional opponent's line. For example, staunch supporters of the "Favorite" party may be unwilling to vote for you if you only run on the Minority Party line. However, if you are on another line, it may not be so difficult for these voters to pull that party's lever for you. You might be amazed how some people, who have voted for one parties for years, if not all their voting lives, just cannot bring themselves to vote for a candidate of the OTHER major party, regardless of how qualified that person is for the position. So, being a candidate for an alternative party gives these people a chance to vote for you without having to sacrifice their "principles".

Primary Elections-

If the options of running with the Minority Party, one of the independent parties (Independence, Liberal, Right to Life etc), or a newly created party do not appeal to you OR if you don't want to wait for years to run with the "Favorite" party, you can try to run as a "Newcomer" with the "Favorite" party. This is done by forcing a Primary Election.

To bring about a Primary Election, you generally must circulate a petition, in New York called a Designating Petition. Each state has different requirements, so you MUST check out the what your state requires. Just like all the other petition processes, you must collect a certain number of signatures on the petition. Generally, only voters registrated with the party having the primary can sign the petition. Additionally, you, too, must be a registered voter with the party. Certain other rules might also apply, for example, the people circulating the petition might also be required to be registered with the party having the Primary. Once you have met all these requirements, the petition must then be filed timely with the County Board of Elections. Again, if no successful objections are made, you become the "official" candidate for the Primary Election. If you win the Primary Election, you then become the "official" candidate for the General Election. If you lose the Primary Election, you may want to go back and reconsider your decision not to run with the Minority Party or one of the independent parties.

In 1995, Cindy and I forced a Primary Election for the position of Town Justice. We followed the above procedure, and it was not as hard as I had anticipated. We got on the primary ballot and began campaigning. We didn't win, of course, but we sure had the opposition running scared. They formed their own independent party ("Good Government" they called themselves) just to assure that they had a spot on the ballot. The ironic part of the whole thing was that Cindy was criticized for flip flopping between parties, but who really was having the identity crisis? Cindy had always campaigned on the slogan that she was "A Justice for All", a judge for all people regardless of their party affiliation.

Another interesting and important fact about Primary Elections is that the campaigning cannot be funded by the party. The Party cannot throw its financial support to its "Chosen One" in a Primary Election.

Funds must come from other sources, like personal pockets. This tends to put the candidates on an even keel financially.

Deciding When to Run-

Selecting when to run and whom to run against are also major decisions in the strategy process.

In New York, General Elections in local government are held every two years (other states may vary). Town council seats are elected for four years and half the council seats are up for grabs each General Election. When you determine the position you want to seek, examine your opponent. Is that person someone who has held the position for a long period? Is that person well liked in the community? Has that person won the previous elections by overwhelming votes? If you're unfortunate enough to meet such a popular candidate, you may not wish to run for that seat. However, if the incumbent is ready to retire, then that's the seat you'll want to go seek. If you know a town councilman is considering retirement in the next few years or is likely to run for another office, for example, run for a town council position one term before the anticipated vacancy. If you do not win, you will have planted the seeds for your next campaign. You will have gotten your name out to the voters. When the position becomes available, run again. Your name will be first and foremost in the minds of the voters.

Another strategy is to run against someone who is not as well qualified as you are for the position. Although this does not always work, it sounds good in theory. If you are an accountant, consider running for tax collector. If you are an engineer, how about being highway superintendent? If you are a CEO of a company, and have the time, how about running for supervisor. If you are an attorney, maybe you would want to be a local judge. This is what Cindy did when she ran. Cindy is an attorney. We campaigned on her qualifications. None of her opponents were attorneys. To us, the choice was obvious, but it took us three elections (and a Primary) to get the message through to the voters.

You should begin your early planning and accumulating tools in the late winter or early spring prior to the next election. In New York, the weather is too miserable to do anything else anyway. As the late spring and early summer arrive, however, you should begin your serious campaigning. The timing all depends on your strategy. If you intend to run in a Primary or form an independent party, you must hit the campaign trail in June or July. If Petitions are not part of your plan, then you can begin your serious campaigning around Labor Day. Whenever you commence your campaigning, it MUST involve AT LEAST the following three components:

-Door-to-Door
-Road signs placed in strategic locations
-Flyers sent to voters at critical times

These minimum requirements, as well as other strategies, must be followed to be successful. These strategies are discussed in the following chapters. For now, lets go see who is at the door…

3

DOOR-TO-DOOR CAMPAMPAIGNING-POUNDING THE PAVEMENT

So, now, you have selected your campaign issues and have the tools necessary for campaigning. Now, how are you going to get your message to the voters? How are you going to convince people to vote for you?

One necessary strategy of any campaign is getting your name out to the voters and making yourself known. Voters like to know who they are voting for. You will find that many people in a community do not pay much attention to local candidates. This is a shame, since the local government more intimately affects the day to day lives of most people, far more than state or federal officials. The "Favorite" Party will most likely be able to get their loyal voters to the polls and hope the other voters remain ignorant and apathetic. This is a great strategy for the "Favorites", which I call "Winning by Apathy". Getting your name out and letting people know who you are and what you stand for provides information to these apathetic voters and encourages them to get out and vote. One effective method to achieve this goal is door-to-door campaigning.

The first time you go door-to-door is scary and intimidating—facing the unknown. As you approach the door, you wonder if you will get the door slammed in your face or be accepted with open arms. You begin to wonder why in the world you ever wanted to be involved in politics in the first place. Suddenly, you find yourself at the door, ringing the bell, when you realize you have no idea what you are going to say to the person who answers. A stranger opens the door and looks at you with the same fear

you are presently experiencing. Now, what do you do? Your initial instinct is to bolt, but your shoes have suddenly turned to cement and now you must say something. I have found that a smile can convey much more than words—it makes the "stranger" feel more at ease and, you feel more relaxed. Before you know it, you have introduced yourself, made your pitch and are walking away, satisfied that you have overcome one hurdle. Now, on to the next house.

In 1993, Cindy and I began the campaign by going door-to-door. We organized a team of 12 to 15 people, who in varying numbers went door-to-door every weekend for about two months before the election. When we first started going door-to-door, Cindy and I were both apprehensive. The last time I went door-to-door was when I was in the second grade selling magazine subscriptions to help raise funds for my school. This type of door-to-door, I had a feeling, was a little different. Nevertheless, Cindy and I accepted the challenge and went out the door, hand in hand. (Your campaign manager may not want to hold your hand. If not, I would suggest you not force the issue!). To our delight, almost everyone was extremely friendly and delighted that we had taken the time to come to their home. As time went on and we became more experienced, the door-to-door campaigning became easier, although the initial fear never quite went away.

As a candidate it will be impossible for you to cover every house and meet every voter personally, unless you work around the clock for several months. This I do not recommend. Aside from the sleep deprivation you will suffer, you will find that most people are not going to be very receptive at 3:00 a.m.! Therefore, you will need others to help you with this aspect of your campaign. Remember those people from the campaign parties? Now is a good time to give them a call (and don't forget friends and family). The volunteers who go door-to-door for you are as important and effective as your own door-to-door, for it conveys the same message; it provides information about you and shows that you care enough to meet your constituents. Sometimes the voter will want to meet the candidate personally. If this should happen, it is imperative that the candidate contact that person, either by phone or in person. I recommend you go to their house personally, it is much more effective.

Aside from the obvious campaign advantages of door-to-door campaigning, there is a more subtle, pleasant personal aspect to this type of campaigning. The relationships you will develop and the experiences you will share with the other door-to-door volunteers will remain with you the rest of your life.

Cindy, when she wasn't going door-to-door with me, either went with her sister, Karen Miltner, or her father, Joseph Farone, who was in his seventies at the time. When we would reconvene with our door-to-door volunteers at the end of the day to discuss the territories covered and the receptions received, we would talk and laugh for hours about all of our experiences. Once, Cindy and her sister came to a house when the occupants weren't home. After leaving campaign literature in the door knob, they turned around and found themselves surrounded by pigs of all shapes, sizes and colors. Not only was finding their way back to the car difficult but avoiding pig obstacles was also a challenge. Another time, Karen was looking for the residents of a country home.

She thought she heard a noise inside the barn, so she opened the barn door and was greeted face to face by a huge ox. Fortunately, Karen has no heart problems and did not suffer a coronary upon meeting her new acquaintance. There were also stories of cows, geese, ducks and dogs, which afforded our door-to-door teams with endless opportunities for exercise as they sprinted to their vehicles. And, there were the many warm and wonderful tales of how the public responded, as well as some stories on the darker side. Door-to-door will allow you to develop special relationships with your volunteers and give you memories you will cherish forever.

Once you have decided to conduct door-to-door campaigning, the next questions becomes, where do we begin?

Handout Material

Before you actually start knocking on doors, you will need to develop handout material. This can take almost any form. The handout is what you will leave with the person who answers the door, or will leave in the door if no one is home. DO NOT put your handout in mailboxes, it is against the law. The handout serves at least two purposes; one, it provides information about you to the potential voter and serves as a reminder that you are running. Two, it gives you something to do as you try to figure out what to say when the person opens the door. People expect something when they answer the door. By giving them your handout you have fulfilled this expectation and put the stranger at ease that you are not there soliciting money or trying to recruit them into a religious organization.

The handout should be short and to the point. DO NOT use a lot of words. People will not read your handout if it takes too much of their time. It will simply be filed in the circular bin i.e. trash. Hit only the main campaign points. Develop something eye catching, like "WHY ARE YOU PAYING SO MUCH TAXES?", printed in big, black letters at the top of the handout. A picture of the candidate is a good eye catcher. People like to put a face with a name. If you decide to use a picture, you will need to have the handout done with offset printing. Photocopies of pictures do not look professional. Voters may not notice if your literature looks professional, but they will notice if it looks second rate. Poor quality handouts convey a subliminal message that the candidate is like the literature—second rate.

The Paper Handout

One type of handout is a paper handout. This can be inexpensive, easy and effective. You can use a normal size piece of paper, 8½" x 11". Colored paper will add pizazz and attract attention, not only for the person you are handing the literature to, but also to other members of the household who may notice your handout lying on the counter top. Remember that the information you put on the handout should be brief. Just because you are using a full size piece of paper does not mean you should fill it up with words. Remember KISS-Keep It Simple Stupid. If you are not using a picture in your handout, you can take it to a local office supply store and have the handout duplicated at a very reasonable cost. Copying can 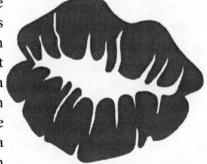 usually be done while you wait. If you are going to use a picture, take you handout to a printer to be reproduced. This is more time consuming and costly, but looks much more professional.

The Palm Card

Another alternative handout is what is called a palm card. The palm card is more professional looking than a paper handout but more expensive. Palm cards are 3½" x 8½" printed front and back on thick card stock, similar to index card material. The card fits in the palm of your hand, hence its name.

The cards are printed three to a sheet and the cost varies from printer to printer. See Chapter 5, FLYERS, for more information on having literature printed. The same rules for a paper handout apply to the palm card-KISS. Hit only the main issues. Using different colored inks to highlight main points is attractive and effective.

Planning the Door-to-Door Effort

Now is the time to use the tools talked about in Chapter 2—your map and data base. You may not have the time or the manpower to hit every house, so you must use your tools to determine the best strategy for going door to door.

The map will allow you to identify those areas—as in your community that are the most densely populated. Target these areas first. The houses will be closer together and will allow you to cover the most houses in the shortest time. Also give priority to those areas with the most voters register with your party. If you have time, you can cover the other areas later. The data base will allow you to target only those houses with registered voters.

(There is a faction which believes that you should target the most densely populated areas last. The belief is that the closer to the election day you introduce yourself, the fresher in the voters mind you will be and the more likely he/she is to vote for you. This philosophy could result in missing some populated areas altogether because you ran out of time. In my experience, it seems that running out of time

AN EXAMPLE OF A PALM CARD

On Primary Day

Vote For

CINDY AMRHEIN

Ballston
Town Justice

"A Justice for All"

On September 12
You Have a Choice

Vote for CINDY AMRHEIN on
Primary Day, September 12
Career in the Legal Profession
•*Admitted to practice law in New York*
State and Federal Courts
•*Partner in the Law Firm "Antokol*
and Coffin"
•*Trial and Appellate Experience in:*
Appellate Division
Federal District Court
Supreme Court
County Court
City Court
Justice Court
•*Experience in Saratoga County District*
Attorney's Office
Education
• *Honors graduate from the State University*
of New York at Albany with Degrees in
Criminal Justice and Political Science
•*Juris Doctorate from Albany Law School of*
Union University
Community Service
•*Coach in High School Moot Court*
Competition Sponsored by the New York
State Bar Association
•*Lecturer at local high schools on legal*
careers
Professional Membership
• *New York State Bar Association*
• *American Bar Association*
• *Capital District Women's Bar Association*

Paid for by the Committee to Elect Cindy Amrhein

occurs with aggravating regularity. Besides, I am not sure that people recall exactly when you knocked on their door anyway.)

In 1993, when Cindy ran for the first time, we did not have one of the major tools needed—the data base. At that time, the cost was prohibitive, so we did without. We went to every house on the street, not knowing whether the residence contained registered voters or not. We probably wasted a lot of time knocking on doors with no voters. Statistics indicate that only about half the eligible Americans are registered to vote, but hardly ever does anyone admit they are not registered. If you should run into an unregistered voter, who admits their error, be sure you have a voters registration form and give it to them. The easier you make it for them to complete the form and register, the more likely they will be to vote for you. I'd suggest, however, that you not go out and seek people who are not registered. This would be a great Boy Scout project, but would require a lot of time with little benefit to you. After all, this is America, everyone knows they should vote. If they haven't voted by now, they probably never will.

1. Sorting the Data

Using your data base tool, print out the data sorted first by street, then by house number. This will provide you with a list of registered voters listed numerically by street address, greatly facilitating the door-to-door effort. Your volunteers will love you for it. All they have to do is walk down the street and knock on the doors on their list. If you cannot manipulate the data yourself, now is a good time to call the computer expert that attended your campaign planning parties.

2. Plan Your Door-to-Door Each Day

It is important to know who will be helping you each day with your door-to-door campaigning. This way you can plan which geographical areas to cover. Each volunteer should be given a list of the streets they are to cover and a copy of the map of that area. Do not forget to give each volunteer a good chunk of handouts. Provide the volunteer with a clip board to help them hold the information and handouts you give them, and provides them with a writing surface. Also, don't forget to give them a pen or pencil so they can make notes or write remarks on the handout for the voters who are not home.

3. Campaigning in Pairs

Your door-to-door volunteers should be sent out in pairs. One person does one side of the street and the other person does the opposite side. This is more efficient since it eliminates the time and danger of crossing the street. It is also safer and more fun for the volunteers to work in pairs. Often, working in pairs this way will result in one person completing their side of the street before the other person is finished. The faster worker may endeavor to help the other person by crossing the street, and hence, confusing the slower worker who does not know which houses to hit. The solution is for the faster worker to stay on his/her side of the street until the end, then cross over and work back toward the second worker until they meet. Try explaining this to your volunteers. Good luck!

4. Keeping Track

Each door-knocker should be instructed to keep track of the houses they visited. When Cindy and I went campaigning, we would indicate an "H" next to the address on the data base list if there was someone home; if no one answered, we would write "NH" next to the address on the data base sheet. This allowed us to calculate the number of voters that were contacted personally.

The volunteers should also keep track of the amount of time it takes for each team to complete their assigned route. This will enable you to determine how many houses you are visiting each hour. This is important. You can adjust your door-to-door strategy depending on how many houses you think you can call on in the time remaining before the election.

During our three campaign tries (and one primary), 20 was the maximum number of houses we were able to visit per person, per hour. This is one house every three minutes. We were only able to do this in densely populated areas. In the less populated regions, the number of houses visited was significantly less. As a guide, I suggest you initially consider 15-18 house visits per person, per hour, in well populated areas, and ten or less houses per person, per hour, in less populated regions. As your door-to-door continues, keep track and adjust your campaign target areas accordingly.

5. What to Say

Practice what to say when you knock on the doors, or you may instantly forget the information the moment you ring that first bell. Remember, practice makes perfect. Instruct your volunteers what to say and how to present the information BEFORE they go out on their assignments. As a volunteer for Cindy, I began with the following:

"Hello, I'm Terry Amrhein and I'm campaigning for my
wife, Cindy Amrhein, who is running for Town Justice. I'd
like to tell you a little about Cindy…"

As I was saying this, I reached out and shook the person's hand, then gave them a handout and proceeded to tell them about Cindy's qualifications. It is important to speak directly to whoever answers the door, make eye contact, and shake their hand if presented with the opportunity to do so. (If it is not unbearably cold, do not wear gloves. This will establish and air of sincerity and friendship.) Since you already have their names on your data base sheet, you may want to address the person answering the door by their name. There are two schools of thought on this aspect; one, the person may be pleased that you know who they are and took the time to come see them; two, the person may be paranoid and wonder how you were able to find out their name. As for Cindy and me, we just stuck with the generic introductions and didn't call them by name.

Instruct your volunteers that if no one is home, they should leave a handout in the door with a personal note like the following:

"Sorry I missed you. Hope I can depend on your vote Election Day" and sign the candidate's name, NOT the volunteer's name. Nobody will know who actually knocked on the door and the volunteers are the candidate's surrogate. DO NOT PUT THE HANDOUT IN THE MAILBOX. Mailboxes are federal property. It is illegal to put anything but U.S. Mail in the mailboxes. You can, however, hang items from the box or the post holding the box.

Before sending your volunteers out to do door-to-door, arm them with answers to frequently asked questions. Some of the most often asked questions are: Why does the candidate want to be elected? What are the candidate's qualifications for the job? What will the candidate do differently? Why should I vote for the candidate? It is not a good thing for the volunteer to stand there with a confused and dumbfounded look when asked a question and respond with, "Da, I don't know". Inevitably, though, a question will be asked that the volunteer will not know how to answer. In that event, the volunteer should indicate that it is a good question, that they do not know the answer, but the volunteer will ask the candidate to get back to them personally. If the resident is really interested, they will supply the volunteer with their phone number and request a call from the candidate. (The volunteer will already have the voter's phone number on a data base sheet, but this should not be made known to the voter. People tend to get a little concerned when they know you have some private information.) The volunteer should take the phone number and write the question on the sheet next to the person's address. This should be done in front of the voter so that the voter can witness that the question is being taken seriously. It is imperative that the candidate get back to that person, either by phone, or more preferably, in person. By doing so, the candidate is usually guaranteed that vote. Sometimes, people will ask the volunteers questions just to antagonize and are not really interested in an answer. If the volunteers suspects that this is the case, they should be instructed to move on and not waste time. This, sometimes, is a tough call. The volunteers should remember that they should not commit the candidate to making lots of calls. Time is precious during the campaign; the candidate and the volunteers are going to be extremely busy during this time. Keeping track of numerous phone calls will put a tremendous burden on the candidate. Remember, the purpose of the volunteer is to help alleviate this burden.

In addition to being armed with answers to potential questions, the volunteers should be instructed, for Pete's sake, not to make promises to the voters. During Cindy's campaign, a few times, some of our volunteers made promises that Cindy could not fulfill. This turned out to be an embarrassment and a bad thing. The volunteers should not commit the candidate to anything that the candidate has not specifically authorized. If someone pushes the issue, the volunteers should be instructed to say that they will consult with the candidate on that issue and someone will get back to the voter.

As you continue your door-to-door campaigning from election to election, you will meet people who are particularly enthusiastic for you. During our last campaign, we met so many people who were supportive and indicated that they had been following Cindy's campaigns over the years. For instance, Cindy's sister, Karen, and I were going door-to-door. Karen went to one house and there was no answer, so she left a handout with a note saying sorry she missed them and proceeded to the next house. Well, there was someone home at that last house, he just didn't answer the door. He picked up the handout and went running down the street after Karen. He said he had been following Cindy's campaign and wanted to meet Cindy. When you meet such enthusiastic people, it is heartwarming and encouraging. Make sure you and your volunteers keep track of those people who indicate that they support the candidate. A list of their names, addresses and phone numbers should be maintained. Such enthusiastic people will help form the basis of your local support, and possibly future volunteers and campaign contributors. This is a golden opportunity to establish a strong support base. These supporters mean you are making headway in making yourself known and on your way to defeating the incumbent. Now, let us take to the road…

4

ROAD SIGNS, OR POUNDING HOLES IN THE EARTH

Road signs probably can do more to get the candidate's name out before the voters than any other campaign strategy. Putting road signs out in strategic places in the community allows the voters to see the candidates name every morning as they drive to work and each afternoon as they return. When they go to the store or out for a movie, there is the candidate's name. When they go to get the local paper, there is the candidate's name. Soon, the name will be everywhere, it's everywhere!

Road signs and door-to-door do a lot toward establishing the candidate's name and her credibility. Road signs tell the voter that the candidate is running for office. Door-to-door allows the voters to meet the candidate on a more personal level.

In 1993, I had no idea how to obtain road signs or how to find places to put them. When Cindy was first asked to run, we had no time or money to get professional signs, so we made them. We bought 1/2" plywood sheets, cut them into quarters, so each sign was 2 feet by 4 feet and painted them. Then we made a large stencil which we placed over each sign and spray painted the words. The message was simple

Elect
ATTORNEY
Cindy
AMRHEIN
Ballston Town Justice

We painted the signs orange with blue lettering. We picked orange because you can't miss seeing a big orange sign on the side for the road, and because orange is an autumn color which goes along with election day. Besides, orange is my favorite color. The dark blue letters contrasted well with the orange background and I like blue better than black. The signs turned out to be acceptable quality although, obviously, not professional. In the following campaigns, we continued using the homemade signs along with the professional signs we purchased. I felt like the voters were used to seeing those homemade signs, so it would give them a sense of familiarity and because the homemade look sort of added a handcrafted, down home, sentiment. Those signs lasted through three campaigns; they are the best buy for the money by far.

Where to put the Signs-

Almost all the signs were placed on private front lawns which were located in heavy traffic areas. I believe it's much better to put signs on front lawns instead of on public right-of-ways, because it makes a statement to the passing motorist that this household will be voting for the candidate. Also, because the sign looks maintained and well kept on a lawn and looks completely unkept in the tall grass and weeds on a right-of-way. In a few especially strategic locations, however, where the private land owner is not obvious, (in an open field with no houses around, for example), I'd place the sign on the public right-of-way.

Try to pick places where the traffic is heavy, on routes that people travel to and from work and on the major roadway through the community. At first, you'll have more signs then places to put them, so you'll have to put a sign wherever you can find a place. However, be alert for better places to put signs. For example, someone may tell you of a good place where you can put a sign. Keep a list of where you put the signs, who owns the property and their phone numbers. With time, this list will grow and then you can pick only the best places.

I started out by calling or visiting our neighbors, friends and campaign supporters to ask permission to place a sign on their property. On several occasions, our friends would know someone at a particularly good spot who volunteered to receive one of our signs. We got permission to put up a sign at the main intersection in town by this "friend of a friend" message system. After I had exhausted our acquaintance list, I started looking for good locations where the residents were Democrats. The Democrats are outnumbered 3 to 1 in our town, so voters who are registered as Democrats are not likely to be squeamish about having a sign placed in their yard. I'd find a desirable location and then look in the voters database to see if I could find a Democrat near that location. If that search was successful, I'd call the people and ask for permission to put up a sign. Occasionally, some people were reluctant to have a "provocative" sign placed on their lawn, I call them the "Closet Democrats". Generally, though, people were glad to help us. Throughout several campaigns, some of these people became strong supporters of our campaign and I looked forward to visiting them and discussing our campaign with them each year.

One other word of advice about placing road signs. Most towns have ordinances about where to place signs, how large they can be and when they can be installed. In the Town of Ballston in New York for example, signs higher than 3 1/2 feet must be at least 30 feet from any street corner and the signs must be at least 15 feet from the curb. Only one campaign sign per candidate can be placed on any parcel of land and the sign must be less than 6 feet tall and less than 32 square feet, i.e 4 feet X 8 feet. Also signs cannot be erected earlier than 45 days before the election and must be removed within 15 days after the election. You can become familiar with the ordinances in your town by asking the town clerk.

Professionally Printed Signs-

Professionally prepared road signs are generally available in two styles; paper signs, constructed of cardboard and coated with a polyurathane, which is supposed to protect against the weather, and plastic signs, having an interior honeycomb construction between two layers of plastic sheet. I have never used the plastic signs but they are very durable and require little maintenance. In the 1996 campaign, the plastic signs that were used survived the entire campaign season with little signs of wear. They seem to be durable enough to be used for several campaigns if there is no dated information on the sign. Unfortunately, the signs are printed using a silk screen method and I don't think these signs can be manufactured with a picture of the candidate.

We always used paper signs because we wanted to have Cindy's picture on the sign. The signs come in several sizes, we found the 22" wide by 28" tall signs to be big enough for the picture to be seen from the road and yet not washed out as larger signs would tend to be. Also, larger signs are more expensive. Unfortunately, the paper signs do not hold up very will in adverse weather, which always occurs in Upstate New York in September and October. The paper absorbs water and loses its rigidity so it bends in the wind. Also, the paper gets soft, so the staples holding the sign together and to the stake tend to come lose. If you plan on using paper signs, plan on visiting each sign several times during the campaign and performing sign maintenance.

Taking Pictures for Road Signs-

Including a picture adds personality to the sign; it lets the voters know what the candidate looks like. If you use a picture, you must supply the photograph. You don't need a professional photographer, you can take the photos yourself with any good camera. Just follow these simple rules.

1) For road signs, always use a light background for the photos. Any other background will not show up well on the sign. If the sign company has to crop the background out of the photograph, the candidate will have that "Darth Vadar" look.

2) Take the photos at several different distances, say from about 5 to 15 feet, to vary the amount of the photo that is filled by the candidates face. Generally speaking, the smaller amount the sign company has to blow up the photo the better the picture will be. However, aim and shoot cameras do not have a focus adjustment and may result in blurry pictures for very close up shots.

3) For women, or men for that matter, don't wear necklaces. A necklace will become fuzzy when the photograph is blown up and won't look good. It will require the necklace to be cut off and result in cutting the picture off higher than you want.

4) Use a variety of expressions, some smiling and some serious, so you can chose your look. Take the whole roll of film. I've been taking photographs for over twenty years and it never ceases to amaze my how many photos I wind up throwing out because something is not just right. You won't have the time to redo the photo session.

5) Use colored film. You can get colored film developed in one hour at most photo stores. Amazingly, many places can't develop black and white photos on their premises and send them out for development. That will take at least one week, which you will not be able to afford.

6) When you get the photos back, you'll have to undergo the emotionally filled task of selecting the best picture. When the candidate

stops to think that thousands of people are going to see her or him by this picture, it suddenly becomes a very emotional event. Usually, you can throw away most of the shots immediately because something is just not right or because there is a better, similar, shot available. It will come down, therefore, to choosing among four or five "best" photos. At this stage the photographer is very vulnerable to complaints like, "Gee, I wish you had done this" or "You should have known to do that". If you perceive that this will be a major problem, then I'd suggest that you have a professional do the work. That way, you can blame all the mistakes on the professional. Eventually, however, the "Very Best", the "Winner of the Show", will be selected. Take this picture, along with the "Runner Up Picture", and have at least six black and whites made from each of them. Black and White photos can be made from colored photos while you wait by using modern scanning equipment and the black and whites will look better than the original. These black and whites will be used for a wide variety of things, so you'll need to have plenty on hand. Of course, one of the black and whites will go along with your order for road signs.

Installing the Road Signs-

Both the paper signs and plastic signs are assembled about the same. Obtain some 8' by 1" by 2" planks from your local lumber yard. Cut the planks in half and saw a point on one end with a circular saw. If you use paper signs, place two of the paper signs back to back, REMEMBER IT TAKES TWO PRINTED SIGNS TO MAKE ONE YARD SIGN, and using a heavy duty stapler (or ordinary stapler if a heavy duty one is not available) staple along the vertical sides of the sign to hold them together. When you attach the sign to the stake, simply spread the sign apart and slip it over the stake. When I first started installing signs, I made the mistake of attaching the signs to the stake before I drove them into the ground. Learn from my mistake, drive the stake into the ground first, then use a staple gun, to attach the sign to the stake. If the sign is attached to the stake first, pounding the stake into the ground will dislodge and tear the paper signs. It's extremely aggravating to see your signs come apart after you've spent a few hours putting them together. Another helpful hint for paper signs is to put a strip of duct tape vertically down the center on the back of each sign so when you attach the sign to the stake, you staple through the duct tape. This effectively prevents the sign from detaching from the stake in the bad weather. If you use plastic signs, you don't have to staple them back to back. Just drive the stake into the ground and use sheet rock screws to attach the sign to the stake. Plastic sign are more durable than paper signs, so you may be able to attach the sign to the stake first, but I wouldn't advise it. One final suggestion on the art of installing yard signs, use a three-or four-pound hammer to drive the stakes. A normal clawed hammer is not heavy enough and you'll wind up wearing yourself out trying to drive the stake into the ground.

Where to Get the Signs-

It's miraculous, but somehow, soon after you become a candidate, you'll start getting brochures through the mail advertising all sorts of campaign paraphernalia, including road signs. The signs come in an assorted array of standard designs and you just pick the one you like best along with your wording. A better alternative, I've found, is to use local stores to buy the signs. You'll have to search through the phone book to find someone who sell road signs. I've found that local stores can get the signs in about one week, faster than through the brochures, and was more economical, about $250 in 1996 for fifty printed signs (which will make twenty five road signs). Many of these local stores can also provide you with lots of help in designing and selecting your sign.

5

DEVELOPING THE FLYER

GRABBING THE VOTER

The best method of getting your campaign message to the voters is by direct mail flyers. Road signs do a great job of getting your name and candidacy out to the voters, but can't effectively be used to present your campaign messages. Door-to-door can help get your message across and to present yourself to the voters, but you will not have the time to discuss the issues in any depth with each person at the door. In a flyer, though, you can present each of your campaign issues in more detail as well as reinforcing your name recognition.

Flyers, however, like the other campaign strategies, have their own set of difficulties. Direct mail advertising is so prevalent today, that many people may toss your flyer into the waste basket without looking at it. How do you overcome this "Tendency to Toss"? Even if you succeed in getting the voters to look at the flyer, how do you entice them to read it? These questions are the same questions that every advertising agency in the country is asking and have not successfully answered. (You'll be rich if you can figure out the answer.) You must also determine where to

 send the flyers. Your voters database lists every registered voter in the town, but many of the voters will live at the same address. Do you send the flyer to each voter, or do you take the chance that one flyer is sufficient for everyone in the household? In addition to these questions, this chapter will address where to get the flyers printed, how best to mail them and how much the flyers will cost.

Bulk Mailing-Meet Your Friend, The United States Post Office

If you plan to use flyers in you campaign, you must consider getting a bulk mailing permit, now called "Presorted Standard Mail". The permit is available from the U.S. Post Office and allows you to mail the flyers at bulk mail rates. In 1999, first class postage is $.33 per letter. With bulk rate, the postage is $.207 per letter if you have at least 150 letters going to a zip code with same first three digits (if less than 150 letters, the cost is $.235). This represents a savings of $.123 per letter. But nothing in life is free; there is a charge for the permit. There are two types of permits. The first costs $100.00. This permit requires that you affix a precanceled stamp to each letter. Sometimes you may want to use this precanceled stamp in your strategy since it makes the flyer look special, not like standard "Junk" mail. Since you save $.123 per letter, this permit will pay for itself if you send out more than 813 letters.

The second type of permit allows you to imprint a bulk rate logo (called an indicia in post office lingo) directly on the flyer, so you save the time and trouble of putting a precanceled stamp on each one. With this permit, you are assigned a bulk rate permit number which must be in the logo. This permit costs another $100.00, $200.00 total, so you won't break even until you send out 1626 flyers. During our last campaign, we mailed about 7000 flyers, so the bulk rate permit saved us $661.

Bulk mailing, however, has some very strict rules to it and the rules are complicated. (The bulk mail pamphlet explaining the system, for example, is over 100 pages long. It's printed on nice glossy paper, though.) Even the Post Office workers have trouble with the requirements. I'd strongly suggest that you talk with the postal people when you get the permit and have them explain what you must do. They are very willing to help you. Some of the requirements that applied are:

1) There must be at least 200 pieces of mail before bulk mail can be used.

2) The mail must be sorted by zip code, which is easy using the voter database, and placed in cardboard trays, which the Post Office will furnish.

3) Arrive at the Post Office with a count of the number of flyers going to each zip code. (The actual postage rate is based on the number of pieces you have for each zip code.)

4) Labels must be printed in all capital letters, if you use printed address labels.

5) The flyers must be mailed from the Post Office where the bulk rate permit was purchased. So purchase the permit in the zip code area where most of the voters reside. That way, your flyer can be delivered from the Post Office to most of the voters the same day you take it to the Post Office.

6) Though bulk rate applies to third class mail, i.e. Presorted Standard Mail, political mailings are treated as first class. This makes the delivery of the flyer faster which is very important if you only have two or three days before the election. Make absolutely sure that the post master at the local Post Office knows it is a political mailing.

7) Flyers which are outside the zip code for the local Post Office, are sent to a central Post Office and then delivered from there. (In our 1995 campaign, 3000 flyers went to Albany where they sat until after election

day. We got dozens of phone calls asking us why our campaign literature arrived a week late. It didn't do much good then!) Arrange with the
Postmaster of the local Post Office to have flyers delivered to other local
offices where they can be delivered directly, or at least determine how to
get them delivered from the central office rapidly.

Mailing to Each Voter or to Each Household?-

The voter database has the address of each registered voter. In many
cases, though, there may be several voters at each address. Should you
mail a flyer to every voter, or just to each household?

During our first attempts at flyer campaigning, we sent an envelope,
with flyers enclosed, to every registered voter. We felt that people might
get offended if a letter wasn't personally sent to them. An individually
addressed letter is also a nice personal touch, which we felt would help
our campaign. In one of our efforts, we even developed one flyer for
Republicans and another flyer for Democrats and other party voters.
What happened in many cases, however, was completely unanticipated.
When several letters arrived at the household all looking alike, the first
one got opened and the rest got filed in the waste basket. Many people
didn't even realize that the letters were different. We even got a few
complaints regarding why we sent out so many letters. This was not the
way to overcome the "Tendency to Toss". It is amazing that the careful
planning of so many people can achieve results that is exactly opposite
to what is desired.

Based on all our trials and errors, it seems that the answer is to mail
only one flyer to every household. However, don't address the flyer to
"THE RESIDENTS AT—", it's far too impersonal. Use the name of one
resident followed by "and family", to "MR. JOHN DOE AND FAMILY"
or, even better, address the letter to "THE DOE FAMILY". If you desire
to send different flyers to voters in different parties, make the flyers
look different. Use different colored pictures and different clip art. Also

send the flyers out at different times. If you're using envelopes, you should make the envelopes look different, using different colors, or send the envelopes out at different times.

There's another advantage to sending only one flyer to each residence; you save money! When we sent only one flyer to each household, we reduced the required number of flyers from 5100 down to 3100, about a 40% reduction. This is probably a typical reduction. With the money you save you can send out another flyer. Two different flyers sent to a household at different times is certainly better then having several identical flyers sent once to the same household.

Mailing a single flyer to each household, however, requires some clever database manipulation from the computer expert that is on your campaign committee. Our rule of selection: only one flyer to a household where everyone had the same last name. If someone at the residence had a different last name, they got a separate flyer. This permitted each person living in an apartment complex, or an adult community, to get a separate flyer, even if they had the same mailing address. It also permitted unmarried couples living together (which seems to be popular today) to get their own flyer. To achieve this selection of households, the database must be re-sorted to eliminate everyone at the given address with the same last name, except the first person listed. The first person's name is used to construct the address label. You see, the services of someone who is very conversant with computers soon becomes a major asset.

Overcoming the "Tendency to Toss"-

Cindy and I had many opportunities to experiment with campaign flyers which I'd like to share with you. The first flyer we developed was simply a letter which included Cindy's picture and told the voters that Cindy thought Ballston was a wonderful place to live and raise a family. The letter also provided information about Cindy and her qualifications. We sent the flyer in an envelope which was addressed by hand to each registered voter. We knew we had to overcome the "Tendency to Toss" and we felt that a hand addressed envelope would accomplish this. Nobody throws out a hand addressed letter! To help prevent the voter from identifying the envelope as a bulk mailing, we used the precan- celed stamps which were affixed to each envelope. These stamps have an eagle printed on them and, unless a person looks closely, it's difficult to identify the letter as a bulk mailing. Sneaky!

The technique of using hand addressed letters, I'm sure, is the most effective method to overcome the "Tendency to Toss". Unfortunately, it takes a long time and a lot of effort to hand address and place stamps on thousands of envelopes. It took four volunteers more than a week to hand address, place the flyers in the envelopes, affix the stamps and seal the 4000 letters. If you plan on mailing out several flyers, this amounts to a lot of time consuming and boring work. Your volunteers may soon mutiny.

In an effort to reduce the amount of toil and hand cramps required to send out envelopes, we eliminated addressing each envelope by hand on our subsequent mailings. We used printed address labels instead. We printed the labels from the voter database using our computer. (Again, the computer expert on your campaign team is invaluable.) We still used envelopes and affixed precaneled stamps to each envelope. This did reduce the time and effort required to mail out the flyer, but the time to stuff the letter into the envelope, to put on the stamp and address label and to seal the envelope was still burdensome. Without the hand written addresses the flyer began to look just like another place of bulk mail.

By 1996, our mailings had evolved into a full fledged flyer just like the bulk mail advertisements we all get every day. The flyer was printed on two 11" by 17" sheets of paper and, when folded in half, resulted in a normal 8 1/2" by 11" size parcel. Printed front and back, it became a four page campaign letter. We provided a space for address labels on the flyer, so when the flyer is folded again, it's ready to be mailed after the address labels are attached. Since we were no longer trying to conceal it as a bulk mailing, we used the imprinted bulk mailing logo, the indicia. And to be even more efficient, we had the flyer folded by the printer. Our volunteers put the address labels on approximately 4000 flyers and had them ready for mailing in only one day!

Of course, now the flyer looked just like any other bulk advertisement. To help distinguish our flyer, and to overcome the "Tendency to Toss" syndrome, we had it printed on colored paper. We used a good quality ivory  stock so it looked like parchment and had a sophisticated quality. Using clip art from our computer, Cindy created an eye catching return address label. (Clip art is thousands of small computerized pictures, like the ones used in this book, that are available from many computer stores. Clip art pictures can be found for almost every subject imaginable. You pick a picture you like and incorporate it into the flyer.) On one of the flyers, for example, we had a picture of an elephant and a donkey writing the word "URGENT" on a sign. Above the sign, were two big eyes forming the word "LOOK". It must have been effective; we won that election.

The moral of this story is, if you have a lot of patient volunteers and some time, use the envelope and hand addressed method. If you're limited by time or volunteers, then use the 11" by 17" bare flyer method. You can also vary your methods, use envelopes for one mailing and bare flyers for other mailings. The envelope method is probably better at getting the recipient to look at the flyer, everyone will open a personally addressed letter. The bare flyer, however, can be nearly as effective if the flyer is designed to peak the recipient's interest and curiosity.

Developing the Flyer-

After you've overcome the "Tendency to Toss", your next challenge is to get the voter to read the literature. If you thought developing an eye catching and interesting exterior was difficult, getting people to read its contents is even worse. What you must do is tell the reader what you want to say without using many words.

Think about it, if you open an advertisement which contains paragraph after paragraph requiring you to spend your time to read and analyze, you're likely to set it aside for a later time or just throw it away immediately. What you must do is use clip art, pictures, labels and short phrases and sentences to transmit your idea. KISS applies here too, "Keep It Simple Stupid" and remember a picture is worth a thousand words. Your goal must be to have the voter read the entire flyer in two minutes or less, and get a good idea of your campaign issues.

Our first campaign flyer, as I said before, contained Cindy's picture, a description of her qualifications and how much she loved the town. We wanted to make it brief, and Cindy's picture was added to provide personality to the letter and to develop interest. The letter is printed on the next two pages for your review. As you can see, there is nothing eye catching, no graphics, no labels, just words. Although it is well written and contains good information, it has too many words.

By our last campaign, we had practice in the art of presenting information without requiring the reader to spend a lot of time. We used clip art to develop interest and present the idea, and pictures to add a little personality to the flyer. An example page from the last campaign flyer is shown on the page following the first letter. This last flyer was four pages long, four times the first flyer, could be read in half the time and was much more interesting to look at. This last flyer is a vast improvement over our earlier attempts.

CINDY'S FIRST FLYER

CINDY AMRHEIN
CANDIDATE FOR BALLSTON TOWN JUSTICE

Dear Neighbor:

While out canvassing door-to-door these past few months, I have had the pleasure of meeting many of you personally. If I did not get to meet you, please let me introduce myself:

My name is Cindy Amrhein. I am a licensed, practicicng attorney who is seeking to serve you as your Town Justice. I graduated with honors from SUNY Albany, with a degree in criminal Justice and Political Science. I received my Juris Doctorate from Albany Law School. I have trial experience in both Federal and State Courts at all levels.

However, a candidate's education and knowledge are not the only criteria for election to office. Devotion and pride in the community are equally important. My husband, my children and I have lived in and loved the Town of Ballston for over ten years. We are convinced it is the ideal community; offering all the advantages and conveniences of city life, yet providing the heart-warming tranquility of a country livestyle. It a community that allowed our children to grow up safely in a peaceful environment, among people who still hold dear traditional values.

It is, therefore, with great honor, that I seek this office. It affords me the opportunity to give something back to the community that has served me and my family so well.

If elected, I will serve with dignity, pride and integrity. The law will be administered firmly and fairly, and I will make the court visible and accessible to the entire community. Is is, after all, your court.

To best serve your community, your Town Justice must know the law. As a practicing attorney, I know the law and keep abreast of the latest decisions relating to statutory and constitutional issues. The law is constantly changing and subject to interpretation and application in each instance. It is imperative that the judge applying the law be aware of recent developments and changes. Only then can the complex legal and social issues of the day be dealt with fairly.

You have the privilege of choosing your Town Justice. Although justices are elected through the political process, they are not as other candidates; they may not take a position on any issue; they may not attack or endorse one another or other candidates; in short, they are to be as non-partisan as the selection of judges by election permits.

Regardless of party affiliation, we all seek the same goal; strong, fair, and qualified representatives. Each of us should carefully examine the qualifications of each candidate and select the one most qualified. On Primary Day, September 12, please search your hearts and minds carefully before stepping into the voting booth.

Above all, PLEASE get out and VOTE!! Thank You.

Sincerely,

Cindy Amrhein

Paid for by the Committee to Elect Cindy Amrhein: Endorsed by the Capital District Women's Political Caucus

<u>CINDY'S LAST FLYER</u>

MEET THE CANDIDATES

CINDY AMRHEIN   **CHARLES MERRIAM**

QUALIFICATIONS

-Practicing Lawyer   -Retired Insurance
                                            Executive

TRAINING

-Bachelor Degrees in: -50 Hour Basic
-Criminal Justice   Training Course for
-Political Science   Town Justices
-Juris Doctorate   -1 day advanced
-3 years full time study   Training Course

EXPERIENCE

-Practices Law in: -Three Months
-City Courts   Experience as Town
-Supreme Courts   Justice
-Federal Courts
-Appellate Courts
-County Courts
-Justice Courts

It is Your Choice
WHO WOULD MAKE THE BETTER TOWN JUSTICE?
On Nov. 5, Elect CINDY AMRHEIN as Your Town Justice
QUALIFIED, EXPERIENCED, KNOWLEDGEABLE

Paid for by the Committee to Elect Cindy Amrhein

During this evolution of campaign flyers, we found ourselves concentrating less on what we were going to say and more on how we were going to present it. Cindy and I spent many hours discussing how we should present information that would catch the reader's interest, what pictures or clip art we should use with the articles and what information we could present that was both interesting and entertaining. One of Cindy's ideas was to present various aspects of the law and explain some of the intricacies to the voters. This would be an educational and interesting article for the voters, and also reveal that Cindy knew what she was talking about and was more qualified than her opponent. How to present the information in an interesting and entertaining fashion for the reader was the problem however. Just describing the law would be really dull and boring. Cindy came up with an idea for describing some of the crimes presented in several nursery rhymes, "Nursery Rhymes in Crime" we called it. We used clip art along with the nursery rhyme and briefly discussed the action and legal consequences of the characters. My favorite was "Pop goes the Weasel"

"All around the mulberry bush
The monkey chased the weasel
The monkey thought in all fun
Pop goes the weasel"

When the weasel popped, as in hit, the monkey, he became liable for an assault charge. The monkey had photographs of his black eye and the weasel found himself in a town court facing a class A misdemeanor. It wasn't fun anymore! The weasel could be fined up to $1000 or one year in jail. I thought this was a clever way to discuss legal issues and not bore the reader. I still laugh when I read these little articles.

In another article, Cindy wrote how non-attorney judges had made mistakes and let potentially guilty people go free. One of these articles dealt with a DWI (Driving While Intoxicated) case in which a drunken driver was allowed to keep his driver license because the non-attorney Town Justice was not familiar with the requirement to suspend the license of accused drunk drivers. DWI is a controversial issue. People are interested in how to prevent drunk drivers from causing harm. When the law is not administrated correctly (and the guilty go free), it stirs feelings of anger in many people.

These same methods can be applied to any campaign. Any contested political election is loaded with controversial issues which interest most people. The trick is how to best get your ideas and thoughts out to the voters. Just writing lots of words won't accomplish the goal, people will not take the time and effort to read them. You must present the information in a clever way, a way designed to capture the reader's interest and curiosity. Use thought provoking headlines, pictures, tables and clip art and as few words as possible to get your idea(s) across.

There are also many subtleties in campaign flyers. For example, Cindy is a young, attractive and very knowledgeable attorney. Her opponents have always been men in their sixties or seventies and not formally educated in law. (We mentioned these disparities in the first part of Charter 2) Of course, we can't say to the voters, "Vote for Me Because I'm a Woman" or "Voter for Me Because I'm Prettier than My Opponent". What we did though, was to publish pictures of Cindy to make sure people knew what she looked like. We knew the opposition would also publish pictures of their candidates, we didn't have to do that for them, so people could see the great disparity of age and appearance for themselves. People make judgements based on appearance, so pictures do help. We were able to point out the significant age difference simply and subtly by using pictures.

Publishing Cindy's picture also helps for those voters who are inclined to vote for a candidate because she is a women. However, in our elections, the female vote was not much of a factor. One might think that being a female would be a great asset. It seems that giving women a chance would be a reasonable change. Cindy was a much more qualified candidate than the incumbent and could fulfill the position of Town Justice admirably. Yet female voters did not come flocking to her side. They voted for the same old tired incumbents of the "Favorite" party instead. It's as though the women don't have faith in the ability of another woman.

The last thing you do, after you've finished your flyer and are satisfied with its appearance and its content, is have two or three members of your campaign committee critique the flyer. Be careful whom you select for these proofreaders. They must be people whom you respect and from whom you can take criticism. They must also be people who are willing to criticize your hard work. It's of no use to get people who won't tell you what they think because they don't want to hurt your feelings. The proofreader should also be someone who will remain your friend after the criticizing is done. Criticism is always hard to take, especially after you've worked as hard as you will on these flyers. During our campaign, Cindy selected her mother and sister. Family members are always willing to criticize and Cindy respects her mother's and Sister's opinion. Also they have little choice about remaining friends. Proofreading is crucial however, because you can very easily commit political suicide by giving your opponents material to use against you, or offend a segment of voters in your political flyers. Your proofreader's job is to prevent this from happening as well as catching spelling, punctuation and phrasing errors. The flyer could change significantly when the proofreaders have finished their review. We had to remove, or redo, entire sections of flyers because our reviewers didn't approve of them. All the while, the campaign manager will be pacing the floor and pulling his hair out because time is wasting. This review must be done, however, so plan for it in your scheduling and be prepared to bear the frustration and anxiety it causes.

Printing and Mailing the Flyer-

While the flyer is being written and reviewed, the campaign manager can busy himself with preparing all the logistics requir ed for the mailing. Bulk mailing permits, envelopes (if used), data base modifications and printed mailing labels must all be ready when the flyer is ready. If you miss any of these logistical items, your flyer will be delayed until everything is in place and the campaign manager will be severely chastised for the delay. So while the candidate is busy writing, the campaign manager must get all of these items ready. The work of a campaign manager is never done!

Of course, a critical item is getting the flyer printed. The flyer should be printed by a reputable printing company. Copying the flyer on a Xerox type copier will not produce the necessary quality, especially if photographs are included in the flyer. Call printing companies found in the Yellow Pages of the phone book and ask for a quote. Make sure that the printer has all the pertinent information he needs to prepare an quote e.g. the quantity you want printed, the size of the printing (8 1/2 X 11 or 11 X 14) and the color of paper to use. Also tell the printer if a photograph will be included and if the flyer must be folded. It usually takes several days to put the quote together. In the 1996 election, I had 3000 flyers printed on ivory colored paper with a photo, including folding for about $250. This was an excellent price and with excellent quality.

Once you've selected the lowest bidder, call the printer and tell them approximately when the final flyer will be delivered. This will help the printer schedule your work so the flyer can be printed faster. Deliver the final version of the flyer to the printer, just as you want it. If there is a photograph, include a space on the flyer and a copy of the photograph, the printer will handle placing the photo in the flyer. Also, if there are several pages to the flyer, such as for an 11 X 17, make absolutely certain the printer knows what the order of the pages must be. Since the pages will be printed back to back, the order can be critical. Include a full size example of how you want it printed.

So, now we've covered the main campaigning strategies. In the next chapter, I'll discuss other smaller, but effective, strategies, some of which can be accomplished with little or no money and with much less effort.

6

OTHER EFFECTIVE STRATEGIES

There are also many other effective strategies which can be used during an election. Although these strategies require some effort, many of these require almost no cost and, therefore, should be used to the fullest.

Press Releases-

Most newspapers will print a press release for candidates as a public service. This means that you should send in a press release to every newspaper which serves your campaign area. An example of a press release is presented on the following page. Send the press release to each newspaper, along with one of your photographs. Hopefully, the paper will print the release and your photo. Viola! Free campaign advertising.

Letters to the Editor-

Letters to the editor are also an effective way to get free campaign literature published. Most small newspapers are hunting for editorials to publish. Larger papers are more selective in how many and what type of "letter to the editor" they print. Many times, however, larger papers will print campaign letters, especially if they discuss an interesting or controversial campaign issue. The same letter should be sent to every newspaper in the area. Although some people may read the same letter more than once, generally people will not read the editorial section in several newspapers, so don't be afraid to take advantage of every newspaper you can.

Not only should you write letters to the editor, but also ask your supporters who live in the town to write letters. Provide them with the name and address of every local newspaper and encourage their participation. These letters can express their support for your political policies, or can just attest to your fine virtues, or past community involvement. If you can get five or six people to write letters and mail them intermittently throughout the campaign, you can easily have a letter or two printed each week throughout the campaign. This helps keep your name and candidacy before the public and shows that you have support.

In some cases, you'll have a timid or busy supporter who would be glad to write a letter "if only they could think of what to write" or "could only find the time". In these cases, write the editorial for them! After all, who knows better what to write about you then you, yourself. If you're modest, then have your campaign manager write the editorial. Ask your supporters if they would agree to send in a letter that you wrote for them and give them an opportunity to edit and change the letter if they desire.

CINDY'S PRESS RELEASE

PRESS RELEASE

FOR IMMEDIATE RELEASE
October 1, 1996
Contact: Terry Amrhein
395-4879

Town of Ballston: Cindy Amrhein announced today that she is a candidate for Ballston Town Justice.

Amrhein graduated with honors from the State University of New York at Albany with degrees in Criminal Justice and Political Science. She received her Juris Doctorate from Albany Law School of Union University.

Amrhein, her husband, and their two children, live in Burnt Hills.

She maintains an office for the practice of law in Burnt Hills. Amrhein specializes in criminal law, real estate transactions and litigation.

If elected, Amrhein will be the first female attorney to sit as Justice in the Town of Ballston.

The letters to the editor should be short; two or three paragraphs is sufficient. Long articles are more difficult to get published. So keep it short and sweet, an introductory paragraph followed by the body of the letter addressing your campaign issues, or providing support for your candidacy.

Personal Recommendations-

Let's face it, a lot of people don't know much about the candidates and really don't know who to vote for. I know before I got involved in campaigning, I knew very little about the candidate's qualifications and policies. Sometimes I didn't vote, but when I did, I wouldn't vote for any of the local candidates because I felt I couldn't make an informed choice. Many other people are like this too. Some people probably continuously vote for the "Favorite" Party simply because they don't know enough about the opposing candidate. If a friend recommends a candidate, however, they're much more inclined to vote for that candidate.

 Campaigning is like selling a product or service for a business, and like a business, word of mouth advertising is the best and cheapest advertising you can get. Don't leave it up to haphazard recommendations, however. Plan personal recommendations as a campaign strategy. Encourage all of your friends and supporters to call, or mail a postcard to, as many of their acquaintances as possible. Friends and supporters don't have to live in the community to make recommendations to voters who do live in the community and can vote for you. After all, a personal recommendation is excellent, whether the recommendation is coming from a the town resident or not. Recommendations should be made throughout the campaign, but are particularly important the last month. Recommendations before that time may be forgotten. Plan to have each supporter call or send a post card to as many acquaintances as they can in the last month. Even if they have already recommended you earlier, encourage them to make another call the last month as a remainder. These recommendations can easily swing a

couple hundred voters over to your side. These votes can mean the difference between winning and losing the election.

Community Events-

It goes without saying that the candidate should attend as many community events during the election season as possible. These events, like church bake sales and volunteer fire fighters fund raisers, give an opportunity for you to meet the voters, let them know who you are and discuss some of your campaign issues. I've found it best if you can get one of your campaign supporters, who is associated with the event, to take you around and introduce you. This works better than just walking up to a stranger and introducing yourself and also represents a personal recommendation for you from the supporter.

Campaign Trinkets-

Campaign trinket (buttons, refrigerator magnets, balloons, pencils and such items) generally are expensive and, I believe, are not very effective for collecting votes. Most of this stuff will soon be discarded. However, if you feel you'd like some trinkets in your campaign, I can suggest two options.

We used campaign buttons. They were metal with safety pins in the back and were very durable, we used them in several campaigns. The cost was approximately $250 for 100 buttons. We would not have been able to afford campaign buttons except for one of our loyal supporters. Cindy's father, Joe Farone, made us an offer we couldn't refuse. He donated the money especially to purchase the buttons. They were bright red, to be easily seen, with Cindy's name on them in big bold white letters. Each of our volunteers wore a button when going door to door. This gave our door knocking volunteers a little more class and helped to alleviate the residents fear that we were asking for a contribution or were with the Internal

Revenue Service. We also wore the buttons whenever we went to a community event. It helps keep the candidates name before the public and helps with campaigning at these events. People will know who your are when you come up to shake their hands.

Another trinket you may consider is refrigerator magnets. Once, we included a refrigerator magnet in each envelope along with our campaign flyer. Each voting household got a magnet. We picked magnets because we wanted something that people would not throw away, something of value. Many people seem to have a difficult time throwing away refrigerator magnets because they're useful in delivering inner-household memos, "Your dinner is in the fridge, Dear" type of notes. Since the magnets go on refrigerators, or another visible place, each household would have Cindy's name staring them in the face for several months before the election. I've even spotted the magnets clinging to refrigerators several years after the election.

Unfortunately, magnets are expensive, they cost about $550 for 2500 in 1995, about $0.22 per voter. It's very difficult to know how much money your campaign treasury will accumulate, so you won't know if you should include magnets within your strategy, or not. Also the lead time for magnets, the time between ordering them and receiving them, is about a month, so, you can't include them at the last minute. They are a good idea, however, if you can afford them. I would suggest, though, that magnets not be purchased in place of flyers, or other prime campaign strategies. If you feel that your bank account is going to be in poverty throughout the campaign, as most campaigns are, then do not include magnets in your campaign strategy.

Newspaper and TV Ads-

Newspaper and TV ads are probably the most expensive advertising you can buy and they probably cover an area different from your campaign area. You'll be paying money, therefore, to cover only a part of your area or to advertise to people who can't vote for you. Either way, the money spent on newspaper and TV ads, in my opinion, is not cost-effective. However, not everyone agrees with me, the most important being Cindy. She feels that ads in Newspapers add credibility and respect to the campaign. She would say, "We may be Newcomers but we aren't slouches". I agree with her on this. Newspaper ads do help add respectability to your campaign. The disagreement was over the expense required to achieve that respectability. It really amounts to your personal style and what your bank account balance is toward the end of the campaign. The nice thing about newspaper ads is that you can run them at the last minute, only a few days notice is required to run a newspaper ad. In 1996, we did have a few dollars available at the end of the campaign and we chose to place ads in the largest paper in our area for three days just prior to the election. I don't know how many votes those ads got us, but I do know we won the election. I also know that those ads in the morning paper cost $370 for three days.

I've spent the last four chapters discussing campaign strategies. However, even the best strategy won't succeed without money. You're not guaranteed to win if you have money but you're guaranteed to lose if you don't have it. In the next chapter, I'll discuss the best ways to get that money.

7

CAMPAIGN FINANCES

How to Beg for Money with Class

No campaign can be conducted without money! I don't care how knowledgeable, righteous, courageous, honorable or friendly you are. Without money you cannot win an election. If George Washington was running for office in today's election system, he would not get elected without money. It's a fact. Nationally elected officials are very aware of this and, unfortunately, many  members of both major parties will accept money seemingly from almost any source. That's one of the reasons why this country needs campaign funding reform. Good candidates should be able to run without such a great dependence on campaign funds. As it is, however, as a candidate, you are dependent upon campaign contributions.

There are many ways to accumulate campaign contributions. Your "Campaign Committee" will undoubtedly have many ideas and plans on how to get contributions. Listen to their ideas, and then forget them! They generally require a lot of organization, coordination and energy, will have little support and will cost more than they bring in.

When Cindy first ran for office, the campaign committee developed a "fine" plan to collect contributions by having a picnic for the candidates. They advertised in the local paper and put up a big sign in the yard where the picnic was to be held. The day of the election, only the candidates showed up. No voters showed up and we collected no donations. We ate our own hot dogs.

Another "Great Idea" was to send out a rousing letter to all the registered Democrats in our community, appealing to their sense of loyally to the party and our strong belief that Democratic officials can be elected if town democrats provide their financial support. The problem with this idea is that it takes as long and requires as much work to develop this letter as it does a campaign flyer. Furthermore, the cost of mailing out the letter probably would not be covered by the contributions which we would receive, so we'd have a net loss for all the effort. Fortunately, sanity prevailed and we did not pursue this idea.

The ideas behind collecting campaign contributions is to collect as much money as you can with the least expenditure of effort. Save your effort for the campaign! You'll spend enough time on that effort alone. So, in my humble opinion, there are only a few worthwhile campaign funding strategies for the "Newcomer" in a local election, and here they are:

1) Use your own money.

2) Ask you strong supporters, friends and relatives for contributions.

3) Have a yard sale.

Using your own money-

Each year Cindy ran, we expended between $3000 and $4000. If you are financially well-endowed, you may be willing to put up this kind of money each year knowing that you probably won't win until your third or forth try. You'll have to shell out $10,000 to $15,000, and may not ever be elected. In my book, that's a big investment for a seat on the town council, an investment which I could not afford. Additionally, most elected town officials in upstate New York get paid only a few thousand dollars each year, so you may never recover your investment, even if you are elected.

Additionally, funding the entire election campaign from your own pocket, somehow seems inappropriate. After all, the local citizens will get the benefit of your services, so at least some of the campaign funding should be provided by the local citizens. It's the American way for campaigns to be paid for by contributions and who, other than Ross Perot and Steve Forbes, should fly in the face of this American tradition.

You will, however, more than likely be required to contribute some of the campaign funds, perhaps even the largest contribution. Early in the campaign, after you've planned your campaign strategy and determined how much money you need, you should start soliciting contributions. When the time comes for paying for election expenditures, be prepared to augment your committee's bank balance with your own money. In other words, don't spend your own money unless you have to. Your own funds should be treated as reserve funds.

Ask your strong supporters, friends and relatives for contributions-

When you first start a campaign you may not have "Strong Supporters", so you will have to rely on friends and relatives. Do not be afraid to ask these people for their financial support, even if they do not live in your town. You'll be surprised! Friends and family will be very supportive of your efforts. First, they probably will not believe that YOU are running for office and they may have never known anyone who ran for public office. They'll be very interested in what you're planning, how you got involved in politics, why are you interested in running and what you expect to do. Don't rob your friends of the opportunity to contribute $10 or $20 toward a candidate that they actually know well. Let them share in your efforts.

We started our campaigns be writing a letter to all of our friends and family enthusiastically announcing that Cindy was running for the Town Justice position. We explained what we wanted to do during our campaign, that we needed lots of money to complete our campaign strategy and requested that they help us by contributing. I think it better that the campaign chairman write the letter on behalf of the candidate and besides, Cindy felt uneasy asking for money. We sent letters to Cindy's relatives and to my relatives. Most of my relatives live in Virginia. We also sent out letters to our friends, who are located all over the Capital District of New York, not just in the Town of Ballston. In a short time, the phone started ringing. People wanted to know all about our election campaign, and asked all sorts of questions. Some of these calls were from relatives we hadn't talked to in years. I had a wonderful time talking to my aunt who called me from Virginia and wanted to know if my "Pretty Little Yankee" wife was going to be a Judge. Soon the bank account we established for "The Committee to Elect Cindy Amrhein Town Justice" started to grow. Almost everyone contributed and the account was in excess of $1000 before we spent our first dollar. Nice!

Obviously, there are a few things you have to do before requesting campaign contributions. First, you have to establish a bank account in the committee's name. If there is a slate of candidates, contributions to all the candidates can be deposited into this account and all expenditures can be paid for from this account. Second, there must be a treasurer appointed for the account. The treasurer, is a very important person because the treasurer must file the required financial disclosure forms.

Failure to file these forms could result in a violation of the State Election Law. Violations of the law are usually not helpful in getting elected to public office so the treasurer must be a conscientious and trusted person. You can find out about the duties of the treasurer from your local Board of Elections and from the state Election Law. (More about the duties and responsibilities of the Treasurer in New York State is presented in the Appendix on the New York State Election Law.)

Several months after the first contribution letter, plan on sending out a second letter to the same people. Your friends and family will not mind sending a few more dollars to help you, but they won't know you need more funds unless you ask again. The second letter I wrote told about the campaign and what we had done with the contributions. Then it indicated what we still needed to do and that we really needed additional contributions. True friends and family take pride in helping someone they know. They would especially want to help a member of their own family, or a good friend, become an elected official. They will contribute if they can and the committee's bank account will be replenished in time to continue your campaign effort.

As your campaign continues, especially after your first attempt at office, you will began to develop a list of strong supporters. People will miraculously appear supporting you. Some will have a particular grievance which they feel you will correct if you're elected or will just have a general complaint against the present town government and support you as a change. Some of these people you'll meet when you go door to door, some will come to you and introduce themselves. Regardless of how you meet, keep a meticulous list of who they are and send them a letter requesting a campaign contribution. The real community support begins when you start developing a list of local supporters. Cherish it, it means you're making headway in becoming elected as a Newcomer. As time passes and as you participate in more campaigns, your list of Strong Supporters will grow but your list of family and friends will not. More and more, your contributions will come from local supporters. This is a good thing.

Finally after the campaign is over, win or lose, you must, and this is a real must, you must send a "Thank You" card to everyone who contributed to your campaign. Tell them what the election results were and include any excess copies of material you purchased with their funds or any newspaper clippings or other media coverage you may have received. Your friends and family will be thrilled to see your name in print and your picture on campaign flyers. Your benefactors deserve to see what their contributions were used for and how hard you worked to keep their trust. These same people will help you with your next campaign so you must treat them well.

Having a Yard Sale-

Yard sales are a great way to increase the balance in your campaign bank account. People love to buy other people's junk. It's also a great way to clear out all of your junk. In our yard sales, we made over $1000 for Cindy's campaign. Ask your supporters to contribute their junk to the sale, too, to increase the quantity of booty. Advertise the yard sale in the local paper and put up a street sign indicating where the yard sale is and be prepared to start receiving buyers at 7:00 am; some people just can't wait.

In our case, we did not advertise that it was a fund raiser because we were afraid it would scare people off. Some people may not come if they think the sale has political overtones or may think it's only for the local community. At the sale though, we put up some of Cindy's signs and wore campaign buttons. It also is a good idea to have some of the campaign literature out for people to pick up.

Plan on advertising and holding the sale for several weekends. What you don't sell one weekend, you may sell the next. So plan on at least two and maybe three or four weekends. When your sales start dropping off, you can make an inventory of everything remaining and take it to the Salvation Army as a tax deduction. Divide the tax deduction up among those who contributed to the yard sale and give them a receipt for their taxes. The Salvation Army is getting very particular about what they accept, so you may have to decide whether to store the stuff for the next sale or to donate it to the trash collector. I personally preferred the latter, but Cindy saw value, or a potential future use, for everything.

Things that Don't Work-

Wine tasting parties, held for seeking donations, don't work unless you have a lot of local supporters you can send special invitations to. These same supporters, however, would probably give you a donation without the wine. Having a wine tasting party, open to the public, advertising it in the local newspaper, will probably only result in having a lot of left over wine or a large hangover the next day. (We did receive a donation of a bottle of wine from a local liquor store for our wine tasting party. The store was operated by a strong member of the "Favorite" Party! The wine tasting party was a flop, but the wine tasted especially good.)

Asking for contributions from the local political party also probably will not be very fruitful. You surely can send a letter to the local party asking for a donation, but, as a Newcomer in a Minority party, expect any contribution you receive to be small.

We've tried asking for contributions from local businesses. However, most businesses will probably be members of the "Favorite" Party, so contributions will be small. If you happen to know of a business that is particularly disgruntled with the present government, a request for a campaign contribution is certainly worthwhile. Be prepared to write a receipt to the business if you are successful.

Collecting campaign contributions while you are going door-to-door, probably is not a good idea. It distracts from the main purpose of door-to-door campaigning, (getting your message out to the voters), and it may offend the residents. It is better to simply note those who seem especially ardent to your door-to-door volunteers, then send them a contribution letter at a later time.

Duties of the Treasurer-

Your treasurer is a special person. She must file the necessary reports, keep the financial records straight, and provide the campaign manager with financial data so he or she can perform analysis on how much things cost. The person must be meticulous and conscientious and must be able to file all the necessary reports to keep you out of trouble. Cindy's mother, Agnes Barile, was our treasurer and she did a fantastic job, as well as being our proof reader, associate campaign strategist and envelope licker.

The treasurer and the bank where the deposits are to be made, must be filed with the Board of Elections prior to receiving or expending any funds. In New York State, the Election Law requires that the treasurer file a report with the Board of Elections several times before the Primary and General Elections and again after the elections. The name and address of any contributor, who donates in excess of $99, must be included on the Financial Disclosure Statements. Expenditures of $50 or more must be itemized along with the name and address where the expenditure occurred and the purpose of that expenditure. The treasurer must keep all records for 5 years from the date the last report is filed. The treasurer must continue filing periodic reports until there are no more assets or liabilities in the account. If all this seems complicated, it is, but the Board of Elections has forms and an instruction manual which the treasurer will receive to help understand all the requirements.

How Much Will the Campaign Cost?-

In order to determine how much your campaign will cost, you must know what campaign strategies you intend to use. Are you going to send out flyers, have road signs, have palm cards? Are you going to place ads with the paper or radio? Early planning and estimating of costs is absolutely crucial to the success of a campaign, I can't emphasize this enough. It is not only crucial for planning your campaign budget, but, also, once your strategy is set, it is awfully difficult to make major changes in the middle of the campaign. You must "plan your campaign and campaign your plan".

For planning purposes, here are some rules of thumb which may be helpful in getting an initial estimate on how much your campaign will cost. You will have to determine a more precise estimate based on your own strategy, situations and location. Most of these estimates are based on 1996 costs, so you will also have to allow for some price escalation for present day elections.

1) bulk postage rate ....$100 if you use affixed stamps (1999 costs)

   (presorted standard mail) ....$200 if you use imprinted logo

2) printing and mailing of flyers ....$0.35 per flyer with a bulk postage rate

3) road signs, paper ones ....$6.00 to $7.00 each ($12.00 to $14.00 if back to back)

4) palm cards ....$0.15 to $0.20 each

5) campaign buttons ....$2.50 each (1995 prices)

6) refrigerator magnets....................$0.20 to $0.25 each (1995 prices)

Ads in the newspaper vary tremendously, you must check with each paper separately.

As a general rule of thumb, we've found that about $1.00 is required for each registered voters in your town. But this depends a lot on your strategy. For example, how many times you send out flyers and whether you send to each voter or each household.

8

PUTTING IT ALL TOGETHER

After reading the information contained in this book, you might be wondering how you are going to keep track of all the work that must be done, make sure that it all gets done on time and doesn't get lost in the hectic pace of the campaign. To help with organizing the campaign, I've developed a very simple Planning Table to assist with managing all the activities. The table is presented below. Please feel free to use or modify the table in any way that suits you. I would stress one principle however, regardless of what planning instrument you use, you must have a WRITTEN plan. Don't rely on memory or develop the plan as you go along! Develop the plan early in the campaign. The work is much too involved and complex to rely on memory and the activities must be completed with proper timing. If you wait too long for some activities you will not be able to recover the time.

The "Campaign Planning Table" below was developed as a planning and scheduling tool and as a financial tool to help you determine the amount of campaign funds you need.

CAMPAIGN PLANNING TABLE

MAJOR STRATEGY: TASKS REQUIRED TO COMPLETE	WHO	HOW LONG	WHEN	COST

Instruction Sheet for Completing the "Campaign Planning Table"

This table comes complete with the following Instruction Sheet to help you complete the table properly and get the maximum benefit from it.

1) List the Major Campaign Strategies. Indicate the date when the Major Strategy must be completed in the "When" column of the table.

For example, one Major Strategy might be to send out a flyer one week before the election so that the flyer would arrive on the

Wednesday or Thursday before the election. If the election was on November 5, the flyer must be sent out on October 29.

2) Below each Major Strategy, list each task that must be completed in order to fulfill the Major Strategy. List the tasks in the order in which they must be completed, use a pencil since you may have to rearrange the order a couple of times to get it right. Next to each task, write "Who" is going to perform this task and estimate "How Long" it will take. Then work backwards from the required completion date for the Major Strategy to determine when each task must be completed. This may sound complicated but it is not. For example, to prepare the flyer, the planning table may look like this:

MAJOR STRATEGY: TASKS REQUIRED TO COMPLETE	WHO	HOW LONG	WHEN	COST
Mailing of last Flyer			Oct 29	
Write the flyer	Cindy	4 Weeks	Aug 30	
Review the flyer, make changes	Review Team	2 Weeks	Sept 27	
Take the photos, get developed	Terry	1 week	before Oct 11	
Get the bids from printers	Terry	1 week	before Oct 11	
Get the flyer printed	Terry	2 weeks	Oct 11	
Print address labels	Terry	1 day	before Oct 25	
Attach labels	Review Team	3 days	Oct 25	
Get boxes from Post Office for mailing	Terry	1 day	Before Oct 28	
Deliver to Post Office	Terry	1 day	Oct 28	

Notice that some tasks can be completed while other tasks are being worked on, e.g. "Take photos" and "Get bids from printers". Only those tasks which are required to be performed in a necessary sequence have a specific date. In this example, you must "Write the flyer", "Review the flyer", "Get the flyer printed", "Attach labels", and "Deliver to Post Office" in this order. One task cannot be started until the previous task is completed, therefore only these tasks have specific dates.

Note also that the dates are the dates when the task must start, not the date when the task must be completed. For example, if Cindy starts work on the flyer on August 30 and it takes 4 weeks, she'll be completed by September 27, in time for the next task, "Review the flyer and make changes", to start. In this way, if August 30 has passed and Cindy is not working on the flyer, we'll know that she's falling behind schedule and is headed for trouble. Remember, Election Day will not wait for you!

Allow yourself plenty of time for the completion of each task. If you feel you could complete the flyer in two weeks, allow four weeks to provide some cushion, e.g. time to recuperate when things go wrong.

3) Once you've laid out the Major Strategies and the tasks required to support the strategies, you can now go down the list and place a cost next to each item that requires money to complete. The costs for items presented in the chapter on Campaign Financing will help you do this. As an example, I've laid out the cost for the flyer below.

Go through the cost for each strategy and you'll know how much money you'll need and when you'll need it.

For our flyer, for example, tasks that require money for 3000 flyers are:

MAJOR STRATEGY: TASKS REQUIRED TO COMPLETE	WHO	HOW LONG	WHEN	COST
Mailing of last Flyer			Oct 29	
Write the flyer	Cindy	4 weeks	Aug 30	
Review the flyer, make changes	Review Team	2 weeks	Sept 27	
Take photos, get developed	Terry	1 week	before Oct 11	$ 15
Get bids from printers	Terry	1 week	before Oct 11	
Get the flyer printed	Terry	1 day	Oct 11	$250
Print address labels	Terry	1 day	before Oct 25	$ 25
Attach labels	Review Team	3 days	Oct 25	
Get boxes for mailing	Terry	1 day	before Oct 28	
Deliver to Post Office	Terry	1 day	Oct 28	$600

TOTAL COST $890

9

ELECTION DAY

THE MOST NERVOUS DAY OF YOUR LIFE

So, it's finally election day. All the hard work, hours of planning and organizing, shaking hands and knocking on doors, writing flyers and letters to the editor, is finally over. Now all you can do is wait and hope that your hard work will pay off. If you're lucky, you'll be able to perform your normal days activities. However, I have never been this lucky. On election day, I usually get out of bed early, because I can't sleep and find that Cindy is lying in bed with her eyes wide open. Once I did try to go to work, but was so fidgety that I couldn't stay seated and couldn't concentrate at all on my work. Fortunately in New York State, there is something you can do. You can become a poll watcher. I believe other states have similar positions. A poll watcher is someone who goes to the polling place and monitors the voting. To become a poll watcher, however, you must be a resident of the community and have a poll watcher's certificate signed by the candidate. The poll watcher certificate is just a form that you can make yourself. Ours looked like this:

WATCHER'S CERTIFICATE

In accordance with section 8-500 of the New York State Election Law
_____(Person's Name)_____is hereby appointed a WATCHER in all
Election Districts in the_____(Name of Your Town)_____for the
General Election to be held on_____(Date of Election)_____.
   Dated:_____
            SIGNED:_____
                                        (Candidate's signature)

With this in hand, a team member can go to the polls and see how things are going. You'll find that people are really very friendly, they'll know about your campaign by now, since you've knocked on their door, and they will be happy to help you.

The candidate, however, is not this lucky. In New York, campaigning within 100 feet of the polling place is prohibited and the candidates appearance at the poll may be considered campaigning. So, I'm afraid there's not much for the candidates to do but sit on their hands, or maybe get ready for the after-election party.

For the other members of the campaign team, however, poll watching can serve other useful purposes besides keeping your nerves in check. As you sit at the poll, you can keep track of who voted by marking their name off on a database listing for the district. About an hour or so before the polls close, RUN, don't walk, to the nearest phone and call those people who are likely to vote for you and have NOT yet voted. In 1993, we organized a team of poll watchers who went to the polls and kept track of who voted. Before the polls closed, we went to our homes and called those who had not voted and urged them to vote. Most of the people we called seemed suspicious that we knew they didn't vote, sort of a "Big Brother is Watching Me" syndrome, so I'm not sure making the encouraging calls is a good idea. I'm sure I did get one person to go out and vote for Cindy though, he was a friend of mine and was just procrastinating.

Even if you don't call voters however, your presence at the polling place can be helpful. A member of the "Favorite" Party may very well be there watching. If they are going to be there, I sure want to make our appearance at the polls as well. I'd hate to give the voters the impression that we didn't care.

There is one thing that you MUST do on election day however. Just before the polls close, members of your campaign team must go to each polling place, with "Watcher Certificates" in hand, to collect the final results. There is no other way I know of to find out the election results on the night of the election. If you don't collect the results, you'll have to wait until the official results are tallied and confirmed, which may take several days. Who can wait that long! The voting officials at the poll will be happy to provide you with the election results but they will not wait for you. So get to the polls early and have one vote collector for each polling place. If you have seven polling places, you'll need seven collectors with seven "Watcher Certificates". This is just a small amount of additional organizing that must be performed.

10

So, It's Finally Over

Since I started this book by explaining why you should not run for office, it seems only appropriate that I finish it by explaining why you should run for office.

As I explained before, you may lose your first election. But even in defeat, it is amazing how many friends you will meet and how much support you will gain. After three election campaigns, Cindy and I have developed some lasting relationships with people whom we would not have met if she didn't run for office. You feel close to these people and they start to become a part of your life. I saw Rod Lowell and his wife Anita, riding down the street on Rod's  motor cycle last week and I waved to them as they went by. I hope that I'm that active when I'm retired. This weekend I saw Nick and Josephine Cristy in a diner having breakfast. They invited my to sit down and have breakfast with them. Nick is world famous in the engineering field because he designed the first rotating restaurants. You may have dined in one of them in some of the larger cities. Last night,

Cindy spend half an hour talking to Hy Agens about politics. Hy works in the radio business, he was a radio announcer on radio station WGY at one time and now works in New York City but lives in Burnt Hills. He's really very interested in local politics and is a wealth of knowledge. Being on radio, Hy can talk for hours without getting tired. After running in a few elections, strangers begin to recognize you from your road signs and they may ask about the election. Cindy went into a local convenience store after the election and the store manager there quipped that Cindy should be buying champagne and not milk.

As a candidate in a local election, you also will have your moment of glory in the new media, especially if you win as a Newcomer. After the election, the phone was ringing non-stop with newspaper reporters. Cindy, briefly, was a mini-celebrity. For a movie star, the notoriety may become intrusive, but for ordinary folks like us, a little notoriety is exciting. We kept our feet on the ground though and never let the momentary glory inflate our egos.

The most rewarding reason for running in a local election, of course, comes if you win. Then you will be able to help enact the policies and methods for which you have been campaigning for and for which the voters elected you. To me, nothing can be more rewarding than to put into place your ideas to help improve your community. You will be affecting other peoples lives. This is a honorable and noble position. It seems that in large elections, many candidates tend to lose track of the reason they ran for office. In small town elections, though, I believe that most candidates are sincere and truly desire to make things better. It is a large obligation. As a Newcomer , the voters elected you to do something, not just to follow the status quo and collect your meager pay. You would not have endured the agony of an election if you did not wish to carry out your ideas. So reap the rewards of being elected and fulfil your campaign promises.

Finally, there is one other benefit from running in an election. Take a vacation, if only for a weekend, and get reacquainted with you spouse or significant other. Believe me, even if you're not the candidate's campaign manager, there will be a long period when the duties of campaigning  will make you like strangers. The reunion will be heaven!

APPENDIX

NEW YORK STATE ELECTION LAW
IN SUMMARY

It is helpful to any prospective candidate to know a little about the election law before you start a campaign. Many candidates find out about the legal requirements the hard way, i.e. by making mistakes. I have summarized the New York State Election Law here. If you live in another state, I'd strongly advise you to become familiar with your states election laws. It is almost certain that your state's laws are not as complex as the laws of New York. New York laws do, however, contain many features which are present in others states.

I'm not a legal expert, that's Cindy's area, but I do know some of the law that may affect you most. If you want a thorough knowledge of the election law, refer to The New York State Election Law. It's over 100 pages long and in many places, trying to understand the law is like trying to solve a brain teaser puzzle. Therefore, short of marrying an attorney, or hiring one to help with your campaign, I hope you find this appendix helpful.

I have not just quoted the election law verbatim, but have tried to interpret the law and present it in a manner that anyone can understand. In doing so, I've left out a lot of words and perhaps have diluted the exact legal requirements of some of the laws. I have tried to present general information for these requirements which is applicable for most purposes. If you have a special situation, needing exact interpretation, then I suggest you consult the Election Law directly.

The legal requirements for elections for a village are different than those of a town, city or county. Also the requirements for running with one of the major parties, is different from running with an independent party. I have tried to present the legal aspects of elections in a fashion that will coordinate the various segments of the election law. To do this, however, I had to rearrange, but not reinterpret, some of the law. This way, hopefully, all the legal information associated with of your campaign will be in one place. I have also added some cryptic and explanatory notes which I hope will aid in your understanding and avoid you having to solve the brain teaser puzzles. I have labeled these notes thusly [Note:...], don't confuse these notes with the law.

The Election Laws in New York City are special, as we all know in upstate New York. New York City law is specifically defined in the Election Law and I have not intended to include any of that specific law in this appendix. This is a book dealing in small town elections, and New York City ain't a small town.

Before I begin, however, I must make the following disclaimer, in true legal fashion:

"The author makes no assertion, either expressed or implied, as to the legal validity of the following summaries of New York State Election Laws. Furthermore, the author takes no responsibility whatsoever as to the use or consequence associated with the use of this appendix. Any use of this summary is done so entirely at the discretion of the user."

Having made this disclaimer, the following legal information may be helpful to you.

First some helpful definitions-

Article 1 section 104. Definitions-

Party-any political organization which at the last preceding election for governor polled at least 50,000 votes for its candidate for governor. [Note: Republican and Democrat are obviously parties, but also Independent, Conservative, Liberal and several others are also parties because of this definition.]

Designation-any method in accordance with the provisions of the law by which candidates for party nomination for public office or for election to party position may be named for the purpose of any election. [Note: "Designation Petition" , for example, is the term used to nominate people for a party. For new local independent parties, which is not a truly party as defined, the term "Nominating Petition" is the correct term, see below.]

Nomination-the selection in accordance with the provisions of the law of a candidate for an office authorized to be filled at an election.

Independent Body-any organization or group of voters which nominates a candidate or candidates for office to be voted for at an election, and which is not a party as defined above. [Note: an Independent Body is what I would call a local independent party. You can form your own Independent Body by having sufficient signatures (5% of the votes cast for governor  in the last election) on a petition and therefore be placed on the ballot.]

Independent Nomination-nomination by an independent body. [Note: To be nominated by a Independent Body you have to have sufficient signatures on a "Nominating Petition" not a "Designating Petition". Designating Petitions are only for Parties. Nominating Petitions are for Independent Bodies. Keeps these two definitions clear in you mind. The law requires a clear distinction between the two.]

Residence-a place where a person maintains a fixed, permanent and principal home and to which he, wherever temporarily located, always tends to return.

Major Political Parties-the two parties which polled for their respective candidates for the office of governor the highest and next highest number of votes at the last preceding election for such office. [Note: This means Democrats and Republicans.]

Caucus-an open meeting held in a political subdivision to nominate the candidates of a political party for public office to be elected in such subdivision at which all the enrolled voters of such party residing in such subdivision are eligible to vote. [Note: This is one of those brain teasers. A caucus is when the enrolled voters of a party in the town get together to nominate their candidates.]

Requirements to Vote in a New York State election

Article 5-102-To register and to vote a person must be
-a citizen of the United States
-18 or older on the day of the election
-a resident of the State of New York
-a resident of the county, city or village for at least 25 days before the election.

If you do not meet the residence requirements, you can still vote for the President and Vice President. [Note: It is useful to carry a few voter registration forms with you when door-to-door campaigning. Any qualified person not registered can easily register by mail in a few minutes.]

Becoming Nominated

Before a person is elected, she/he must be nominated. The process of being nominated is presented in the topics below. The process is

different if you're nominated by party caucus or by party primary. In general, the process for a party primary consists of:
-collecting signatures on a designating petition
-filing the designating petition
-filing the certificate of acceptance of the designation
-filing and presenting any objections to the designation, acceptance or nomination
-having a primary election
-having the general election.

If you're nominated by party caucus, the process is easier because there is no primary election. But you still have to file the certificate of acceptance of nomination made by caucus and possibly deal with objections.

The process is also different if you're starting a new "independent body". For the independent body the process is
-collect signatures on the nominating petition
-filing the nominating petition
-filing the certificate of acceptance for the nomination, (for a new independent body, there is no primary)
-filing and presenting objections
-having the general election.

Party Nominations for Towns-

Article 6-108: 1. If the town population exceeds 750,000, as determined by the last census, the nomination must be done by a primary vote. Any other town nomination can be done by primary or caucus.

2. Notice of a town caucus must be given by newspaper between one and two weeks before the caucus OR by posting notices in at least 10 public places at least 10 days before the caucus.

To participate in the town caucus, a person must be enrolled in the party and a registered voter in the town.

Article 6-118: A designating petition must be used for party primaries to designate candidates for a party nomination or to nominate a candidate for a party position. [Note: The designating petition can be used to force a primary election for a party position as well as for an elected office.]

Article 6-120: A person designated in a designating petition must be an enrolled member of the party at the time of filing the petition or must have authorization from that party. This does not apply to political parties nominating candidates for the first time, to candidates nominated by caucus or to candidates for judicial office. [Note: Candidates for a judicial office are not required to be enrolled in the party holding a primary. This is because judicial candidates are not supposed to have strong allegiance to any party.]

Article 6-122: A person designated or nominated for a public office must be a citizen of the State of New York, be eligible to be elected and can meet the statutory qualifications for the position.

Rules for Designating Petitions, for Towns, Cities and Counties-

Before starting your petition drive you must obtain an identification number. You can obtain the number by providing a written request to the County Board of Elections.

Article 6-130: The designating petitions must include the full name of the signer, his residence address, the election district, name of the town or city and the date of signature. [Note: Designating petitions in the correct format are available at the Board of Elections.]

Article 6-134: Designating petitions can designate candidates for one or more public offices, or one or more party positions. Designating petitions shall be bound together, sheets shall be numbered and a cover sheet attached. [Note: The Board of Elections can provide the exact format of the petitions.]

Signatures on the designating petition must be made within 37 days before the last date for filing the petition. [Note: Designating petitions must be filed with the county Board of Elections between the tenth Monday and the ninth Thursday before the primary. The ninth Thursday therefore is the last day to file the petition. So all signatures on the petition must be made within 37 days before this ninth Thursday. The county Board of Elections will provide a calendar which has all the important dates listed. This will save you from having to figure out the dates yourself. Nominating petitions for "Independent Bodies" must also be filed with the county Board of Elections on a different date.]

Alterations made to the petition, except for the signature and date, will not invalidate the signature. The signer needs only to sign the petition, he need not complete the remaining information.

Article 6-136: The number of people required to sign a designating petition is 5% of the enrolled voters in the party of the town, (city or county) except the signatures need not exceed:

-2000 signatures if the inhabitants exceed 250,000
-1000 signatures if the inhabitants is between 25,000 and 250,000 or
-500 signatures if the inhabitants are less than 25,000
-1000 signatures for any state senatorial district
-500 signatures for any state assembly district
-500 signature for any county legislative district

Filing Dates for Designating Petitions and Caucus Nominations-

Article 6-158: Designating petitions shall be filed between the tenth Monday and the ninth Thursday before the Primary Election. [Note: The primary election is set by law as the first Tuesday after the second Monday in September.]

A certificate of acceptance (or decline) of the designation must be filed before the fourth day after the last day to file the designating petition, [Note: This means you have four days to file the acceptance after the last day to file the petition.]

A certificate of party nomination made by caucus must be filed within seven days after the date of the primary. The certificate of acceptance (or decline) for the party nomination must be filed within three days after filing the party nomination.

Rules for Nominating Petitions for Independent Bodies-

Article 6-138: 1. Independent nominations for a public office must be made by petition. Signatures on the petition must be made by voters in the community who are registered prior to the first day allowed for signing the petition. [Note: Since this is an independent party, members of any party can sign the petition provided they have not signed any other petition for that office.]

2. The form and rules for the nominating petition are the same as the designating petition. The name of the new party shall not include the name of another existing party. The emblem of the new party shall not be similar to the emblem of an existing party.

3. Signatures made six weeks before the last date for filing the petition will not be counted.

Article 6-142: The number of voters required to sign an independent petition shall be 5% of the total number of votes cast in the community for governor at the last gubernatorial election except not more then 3500 signatures are required.

TIME LINE FOR DESIGNATING AND NOMINATING PETITIONS

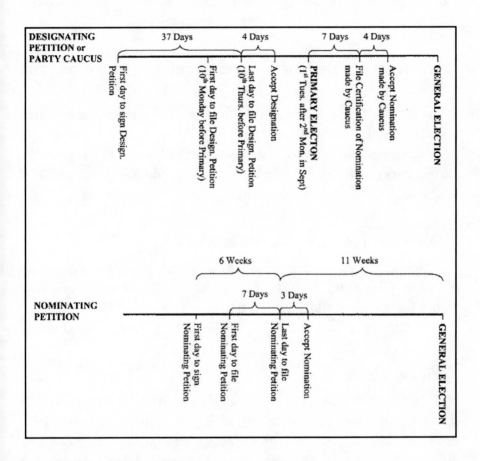

Filing Dates for Nominating Petitions-

Article 6-158: Petitions for an independent nomination must be filed between 11 and 12 weeks before the General Election.

A certificate of acceptance of an independent nomination must be filed before three days after the eleventh Tuesday preceding the General Election. [Note: The petition must be filed by the eleventh week before the General Election and the General Election is on a Tuesday. The acceptance, therefore, must be filed by the Friday after the last Tuesday that the petition can be filed. I love the brain teasers.]

Where to file Designating and Nominating Petitions and Certificates-

Article 6-144: Petitions and Certificates shall be filed in the county Board of Elections office.

For a village election, petitions and certification shall be filed in the village clerks office, if the election is not conducted by a Board of Elections.

Objections to Petitions or Certification-

Article 6-154: Any registered voter can object to any petition or certification. Objections must be filed in the Board of Elections office within three days of filing the petition or certification. The specifics of the objection must be filed within six days after filing the objection.

Village Elections-

Village elections are governed by a different article than town or city elections. The rules governing designating petitions, nominating petitions, the dates for filing petitions, accepting nominations etc. are all different. The date of the General Election is even different. Below is a summary of the regulations governing villages:

Article 15-104: The general village election shall be held on the third Tuesday in March unless the village adopts a proposition to elect its officers on a different date.

Party Nominations in Villages-

Article 15-108: Party nominations in villages can be done by caucus or by party primary.

Party primaries must be held 49 days before the general village election.

Notice of a primary must be given in at least one general circulation newspaper at least once in each of the two weeks preceding the primary.

Notice of a caucus must be given in a newspaper at least once within one to two weeks of the caucus or by posting notices in at least six publics places at least 10 days before the caucus.

Notices shall provide the time and place and purpose of the caucus or primary and shall contain the offices for which candidates shall be nominated.

No person shall participate in a caucus or primary unless they are
-a resident of the village and
-an enrolled voter in the party conducting the caucus or primary

Party nominations made by caucus or primary shall be filed with the village clerk.

Designation Petitions for Villages-

Article 15-108: Signatures on designating petitions shall be made in ink by residents of the village who are registered voters and are enrolled in the party. Signatures shall be made within six weeks of the last day to file the petition.

The number of signatures required on a designating petition shall be 5% of the number of enrolled voters of the party residing in the village.

Designating petitions for a village primary shall be filed with the village clerk between 22 and 15 days before the primary election.

A certificate of party nomination shall be filed between 54 and 47 days before the general village election. [Note: Since the primary must be held 49 days before the village election, a certificate of nomination must be filed within two days after the primary, if a primary is held.]

A certificate of acceptance (or declination) of the nomination must be filed not later than 44 days before the general village election. [Note: You have three days to accept the nomination after the last day to file the certificate of party nomination.]

Written objections to a petition or a certificate of nomination shall be filed in the village clerk's office within one day of the last day to file the petition or the certification of nomination. The specific grounds of the objection shall be filed within two days following the objection.

Independent Nominations-

Article 15-108: Signatures on independent nominating petitions shall be made in ink by residents of the village who are registered voters. Signatures shall be made within six weeks of the last day to file the petition.

The name of the independent body shall not include the name of an existing party.

The independent nominating petition for a village office shall contain the names of

-at least 100 voters if the village population is 5000 or more

-at least 75 voters if the village population is between 5000 and 3000

-at least 50 voters if the village population is between 3000 and 1000

-and 5% of the number of voters at the last village election if the village population is less than 1000.

Independent nominating petitions shall be filed between 42 and 35 days before the general village election.

A certificate of acceptance must be filed within 3 days after the last day to file the petition.

Written objections to a petition or a certificate of nomination shall be filed in the village clerks office within one day of the last day to file the petition or the certification of nomination. The specific grounds of the objection shall be filed within two days following the objection.

TIME LINE FOR VILLAGE PETITIONS

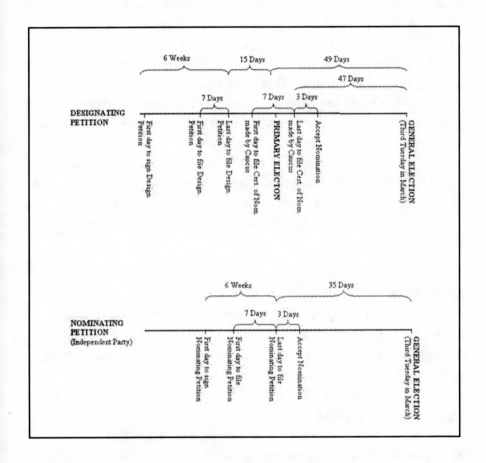

Conduct of the Election-

Article 8-100: Primary elections are held on the first Tuesday after the second Monday in September.

Polls for a primary election are open from 12:00 noon to 6:00 p.m. Polls for a general election are open from 6:00 a.m. to 9:00 p.m.

Article 8-102: Election Inspectors are charged with maintaining order in the polling place and with assuring the election is conducted in accordance with the laws.

Article 8-104: No campaigning can be conducted within 100 feet of the entrance of the polling place. No political signs, buttons, poster etc. can be present within this 100 feet distance.

Article 8-500: At any general or primary town or village election, any party or independent body may have up to three poll watchers present to observe the processing of the election.

Watchers shall be appointed by a written certification issued by the party or independent body chairman or by a candidate. [Note: See the chapter on "Election Day" to obtain the form of the certificate.]

Each watcher must be a qualified voter in the city or county in which he/she is serving.

Rules for Treasurer-

Article 14-118: All political committees shall have a treasurer. No contributions can be collected and no expenditures made until the committee has selected a treasurer and has chosen a New York State bank and has filed this information with the Board of Elections.

The name and address of the treasurer and all other people authorized to sign checks and the name and address of the bank where the committee has established an account must be filed with the Board of Elections within 5 days after selection.

Duties of the Treasurer-

Article 14-102: The treasurer of every political committee shall file a sworn statement identifying all contributions to the committee and expenditures by the committee.

The statements shall include the amount of the contribution, the name and address of the contributor and the date of the contribution. For expenditures, the statement shall provide the amount of the expenditure and the name and address where the expenditure was made, the date of the expenditure and the purpose of the expenditure.

Expenditures of less the $50.00 need not be specifically accounted for. Contributions of $99.00 or less need not be specifically accounted for in the statement of contributions.

Article 14-108: Dates for financial statements shall be determined by the Board of Elections but shall be filed for any general, primary or special election. Statements shall be filed

-between 30 and 45 days before the election

-between 11 and 15 days before the election and

-after the election [Note: the time of the filing after the election is not specified.]

Also, statements must continued to be filed every six months, until the committee goes out of business.

Statements must be correct to within four days of filing the statement, except contributions in excess of $1000 must be reported within 24 hours.

Statements must be preserved by the treasurer for 5 years after the date the last financial statement was filed.

Article 14-110: The state Board of Elections shall determine where the statements must be filed. [Note: The statements are generally filed with the county Board of Elections.]

Article 14-118: Contributions in excess of $100 must be made by check and made payable to the candidate or political committee.

No expenditure in excess of $100 can be made except by check drafted from the designated bank and signed by an authorized person.

Article 14-122: All expenditures and contributions must be reported to the treasurer within 3 days.

All expenses greater than $10, shall have a receipt stating the purpose for the expense.

Article 14-128: All anonymous contributions shall be turned over to the State of New York for use in the general treasury of the state. [Note: I'll bet there are very few, like zero, anonymous contributions!]

Article 14-130: No campaign funds can be used for personal use.

Maximum Allowed Contributions-

Article 14-114: The maximum contribution that is allowed to be made by any one contributor to a candidate or political committee is
   -for party position or for nomination: $.05 multiplied by total number of enrolled voters in the candidate's party in the district but not less than $1000 or greater than $50,000,
   -for election for an office: $.05 multiplied by the total number of registered voters in the district but not less than $1000 or greater than $50,000
However, the candidate's children, parents, grandparents, brothers and sisters and spouse can contribute
   -for party position or for nomination: $.25 multiplied by the total number of enrolled voters in the candidate's party in the district but not less than $1250 or greater than $100,000,
   -for election for an office: $.25 multiplied by the total number of registered voters in the district but not less than $1250 or greater than $100,000.
[Note: This paragraph of the article is one sentence, 58 lines long. It has a lot of commas, however, so the reader can take a breath.]

The limits on the amount of contributions will be adjusted using the consumer price index in the fourth quarter of each year starting in 1995.

Contributions made to a political party supporting more than one candidate, shall be allocated among the candidates in a reasonable fashion.

A loan made to a candidate which is not repaid by the date of the primary or general election, shall be considered a contribution.

ABOUT THE AUTHOR

For over twenty five years, Terry Amrhein has been an engineer and project manager for the General Electric and Lockheed Martin Corporations. Becoming a campaign manager for his wife in a small town election was natural for Terry who has years of experience in organizing and developing all sorts of projects. After three campaigns, Terry helped his wife become the first "Newcomer" elected in their town in over twenty years. This book tells how he did it!

LaVergne, TN USA
07 February 2010
172299LV00002B/245/A

9 780595 009916